The Matrimandir Gardens and Nursery
a sequence of development

Narad

Copyright : Prisma, Auroville
Author : Narad

First edition: 2023

ISBN 978-93-95460-64-4 (Paperpack)
ISBN 978-93-95460-69-9 (ebook)

BISAC Code:
GAR000000, GARDENING / General
GAR006000, GARDENING / Garden Design
GAR018000, GARDENING / Reference
NAT026000, NATURE / Plants / General
ARC008000 ARCHITECTURE / Landscape
NAT013000, NATURE / Plants / Flowers
HIS000000, HISTORY / General

Thema Subject Category:
WM, Gardenings
WMB, Gardens (descriptions, history etc)
WMD, Garden design and planning

Cataloging-in-Publication Data for this title is available from the Library of Congress.

Published by:
PRISMA, an imprint of Digital Media Initiatives
PRISMA, Aurelec / Prayogshala,
Auroville 605101, Tamil Nadu, Indiaa
www.prisma.haus

"Ah, this is it"
The Matrimandir Gardens – a sequence of development

Introduction

The following is a collection of various notes, letters, articles and photos on the Matrimandir Gardens and their surrounding area, compiled essentially in date order. They include pieces not strictly relating to the Gardens, but personally relevant to me (Narad) and to life in Auroville at the time.

However, not all of them were written by Aurovilians. Examples are correspondence with Ashramites, letters from the Government's Forestry Department, pieces contributed from the diary of a visitor who spent seven weeks in 1973 in the area with his wife and two children, and pieces relating to people further afield. All combined together they contribute to a more complete and wider perspective on the period to date and life in and around the Matrimandir site, the Matrimandir Nursery and the Gardens.

Home, and an invitation

I have returned to Auroville - my soul's home - and to the Matrimandir Gardens, who have called me to complete the work given me by the Mother. There are eight gardens still to be brought down, and they are ready to manifest if we can find in our collective soul the harmony that will entice them to descend.

We can no longer rely on the inadequacy of mind with its thousands of conflicting propositions nor on the vital nature with its inordinate desires and its insistence on its way. Our need is to open to the Divine Force and allow it to guide us in the manifestation of the Gardens, which Mother has said are as important as the Matrimandir itself. In Auroville, who is willing to contribute?

There are many Gods willing to help in this work of works, rain gods, sun gods, the gods and fairies of flowers, the gods of the earth, and more, but we must consciously and willingly invite their presence.

I call on all souls in Auroville who are ready to contribute whatever time and energy they can to make this work one of collective harmony and realization, where the Supramental will be felt in all beings and the sense and love of aesthetic beauty will be evident to all on entering the Gardens.

We went up to Mother on my partner Anie's birthday, December 18th, and it was at this time that Mother spoke to me of the Gardens. Her voice was so strong and so clear! She said, "It must be a thing of great beauty - of such a beauty that when men enter they will say, 'Ah, this is it!' and they will experience physically and concretely the significance of each Garden. In the Garden of Youth they will know Youth. In the Garden of Bliss they will know Bliss, etc." Then She raised Her hand and said, "One must know how to move from Consciousness to Consciousness."

Before we left She said, "It must manifest something of that which we are trying to bring down", and added, "I would like you to begin with the Garden of Unity".

Dear Aurovilians, will you collaborate with me in love and harmony?

Narad

9 January 1969

Matrimandir Gardens and Nursery - various documents

[Mother gives the following message to Arindam for the people living in the area previously known as "the Centre", which she had named "Peace" on 29th December 1968:]

"Peace". The foremost thing must be Peace. Whatever you do must be by peaceful means. The second thing necessary is Harmony, not only general harmony but also between the individuals living there. You must begin to look for the harmony in each individual and not dwell on the disharmony. The disharmony exists everywhere but you must reject that and allow only the harmony to enter. There must be a sense of Order. Each individual must have a sense of self-discipline, and actually practice it.

PEACE, HARMONY, ORDER, SELF-DISCIPLINE.

Early 1969

Frederick in the interview "Looking Forward, Looking Back"
[According to Frederick, Mother said:]
There is nothing living at the Centre, there is nothing to receive my Force, and I want you to plant some trees.

Around 1970

Guidelines for landscapers of the Matrimandir Gardens

The space between the Oval Road and the 12 Petals which houses the 12 Meditation Rooms consists of 5 areas:
- a 5,000-seat open air amphitheatre,
- a 300-seat open air mini-amphitheatre,
- the Garden of Unity, between a large Banyan tree and the mini-amphitheatre,
- the Inner Park and
- the 12 Matrimandir Gardens.

The 12 Gardens are meant to express 12 states of consciousness which are defined in the annex, and the landscaping must help the visitor "to move from consciousness to consciousness". For each Garden, one plant has been defined as being its main resident. It often belongs to the hibiscus family. Other plants and flowers may be added.

The Matrimandir wants to be the symbol of the Universal Mother, according to Sri Aurobindo's teaching. In the same manner, the states of consciousness to be manifested in the 12 Gardens are those which are described in the works of Sri Aurobindo and the Mother.

A global invitation for the design of the Garden of Unity and the 12 Gardens is extended to everybody who is receiving some higher intuition. The landscaping must not be a mental construction but an outcome of the right inspiration.

It is recommended that landscapers who are interested to participate in the designs of one or more gardens visit Auroville and Matrimandir first for a good understanding of Matrimandir and the requirements of the Gardens.

After perusal of their former projects and examination of their reflections on the specific theme(s) they have selected for one or more Gardens, designers may be invited to present three or four sketches to be scrutinised by a Panel who will bring comments and orientations. The next step will be to present a model at 5 mm/m to the Panel.

If the applicant is willing to work for improvement of his concept according to the recommendations of the Panel, some indemnity will be given to allow him to continue working on the model.

If the concept is retained for execution, some fees will be paid to the landscaper and his design will become the collective asset of Matrimandir. No landscaper will remain the owner of his concept. It means that every designer is ready to hand over his proposal to the Panel and work in close contact with one or several other persons. This principle should allow any new intuition/inspiration to replace an existing concept. The design must be open for a permanent evolution.

A prototype in situ will first be built with cheap materials in order to develop the shapes, the volumes, and to have an idea of the association of different colours and to position the flowers, the plants and the minerals.

(Undated)

On the designs of the next four Matrimandir Gardens

I have seen many beautiful gardens in the world, from Canada, the United States, Thailand, India, Japan and many more. They are beautiful gardens, often creative masterpieces (I don't refer to severely clipped forms or those of animals, etc, which is a gross distortion of Nature), but those with a vision that endures the toll of time.

It will take designers who are essentially open to the Divine Vision, mostly egoless and humble, and dedicated to the manifestation of supreme beauty. In addition they must be able to catch the Force that wants to descend and surround the Matrimandir.

Narad with Marie, one of the designers of the Matrimandir Gardens

As I have previously written, Mother said,
"The Gardens are as important as the Matrimandir".

With my love to all

And my prayers,

Narad

January 1970

Letter from Huta

My dearest Mother,

Richard Eggenberger is grateful to You for Your kind blessings.

He is going to start his work of taking the slides of the whole of Savitri.

He came to me today and told me that he could spend more and more time in this work of Savitri if he has no more work of gardening in Auroville. He expressed his feeling that he is more inclined to the art and music and he wishes to do something in the slides of Savitri.

I wish greatly that this work of Savitri should be done wonderfully with the new inspiration. So I pray to You, Mother, please allow him to take up this new work of slides taking and showing with Your recitations and with the new music.

Mother, let this work spread more and more all over the world - let people open themselves to Savitri.

Please do the needful.

Richard wishes to have Your answer regarding this work.

Love

Yours Huta

> **[Mother replies:]**
> It is all right, he can do this work at the best of his capacity.
> But he must make arrangements so that the gardens of the Matrimandir will not suffer.
> Blessings

10th June 1970

Mother finishes working with Tara on Her commentaries of Sri Aurobindo's "Thoughts and Aphorisms". From now onwards Tara, together with Richard P. and Narad, will assist Mother in the thorough revision of Lizelle Raymond's flower book.

From June 1970 to April 1972, Mother will see hundreds of flowers, change some names, confirm others and name flowers She hadn't yet named. Mother will also give a commentary for each one of the flowers (except for the last one: "Controlled Power"). Tehmi does the translation into English and the next day she checks certain translations in cases of new flowers.

The book "Flowers and Their Messages" will be published in August 1972 by Auropress, at Auroville. This is the last book on which Mother worked.

By revising this book, naming new flowers and giving a commentary for each flower, Mother obviously enriched the dictionary which enables us to understand better the messages and teaching of flowers. Flower games have thus become much more interesting.

(Undated)

Anie's letter and Mother's reply

Narad,

Here is a copy of a dream experience during my days at the Nursery. It was sent to Mother and I have also enclosed Her response.

Where is the dream experience and Mother's reply?

Her answer certainly seems to underscore the importance of the work of the Nursery and Gardens.

Those trees and plants now surrounding the Matrimandir stand as living symbols of all the love, consciousness and care that went into the planting of those initial seedlings by the early pioneers of Auroville. As I see it, they imbibe the very Force and Presence of the Mother.

In Her Light,
Anie

early 1970's

Narad recounted this dream to Vladimir at Savitri Bhavan.
After a moment he quoted this line from Savitri:
"A branch of heaven transplanted to human soil".

Undated

Article - The Spirit of Auroville

[Narad's account of how Mother called him to start the Gardens of Matrimandir:]

It was in 1969 that Mother informed me through one of her secretaries [Udar] that She wanted me to prepare to come and develop the gardens of Matrimandir. I wrote to ask Her how to prepare for that great work. She replied that a combination of studies and practical work was best. And suddenly, everything opened before me! Teachers came, constructive

opportunities... In the autumn of 1969 I received the most wonderful surprise from the Mother, in her own hand:
"A Bientôt - 18 December 1969"

3 April 1970

Letter signed by Anie and Narad
To give some background on how we became connected with the Auroville gardens, and when and how the Mother gave this vast work, I shall go back to 1968 just after the inauguration of Auroville. Narad and I were receiving Darshan of the Mother shortly before his return to America. Mother looked very deeply into him and said...

"Don't you want to come for Auroville, I feel you can do something there?"

Of course Richard's answer was yes.
After his return to America there was a period of intense inner work and much correspondence with Mother, the result of which revealed to him his work: that of designing Mother's gardens for the City of Auroville. Mother told him to prepare for this work by gaining knowledge and experience, but not to approach the work from a mental standpoint, rather, to allow the Force to work through him. He ultimately gained much experience in the California area, studying horticulture, plant combination theory and design at UCLA.
Mother wrote...
There are now two Americans here, husband and wife [Richard and Anie], and the husband studied there for more than a year the art of gardening, and he came here with that

knowledge. So I asked him to start straight away preparing the plan for the inner garden; they're working on it.

But then, the answer is always the same: "We have no money!"

29 June 1970

Newsletter to friends
Report: Matrimandir Gardens

It is now more than two months since the first report was written as to the progress of the Matrimandir Gardens, and much has developed in the intervening weeks. To date, nothing concrete has begun toward the design and execution of the Garden of Unity (the garden with which the Mother had asked us to begin our work) due to the fact that all the land covering that area has not yet been purchased, nor has the electricity which we were promised last February been installed as yet. This latter inconvenience means that there is still no water at the center, and consequently prevents any further planting in the vicinity of the Urn and the surrounding area. However, much work has been accomplished in the Nursery of the main gardens and we have made many experiments which have proved to be valuable to the work.

In the beginning of April Mother sent a new worker, Don Cox from America. He has had some experience as a landscape foreman, but is now no longer with us as he has started to drive the tractors for Auroville. The Tamil boy, Radhakrishna, has also left the Nursery in order to gain experience in Auro Garage, and Dirk, the Dutch boy, is on a world tour. We now have four people working regularly with Howard, myself,

Richard and Jean, an American girl who previously lived in the Ashram and worked in the Press.

We accomplished much in the days prior to the brief visit of [American] Ambassador Olds and his wife on April 15th. Richard purchased sod from the botanical garden, and from the edge of the brick patio extending to the incline where Howard built a stone wall the sod was placed into the ground. It was quite an event, and many village men joined in a spontaneous offering to help as most had never seen this type of work done before. The grass is thriving now, even during these weeks of intense heat, and lends a cool and refreshing atmosphere to the Nursery. The biggest project in the month of April was the laying of the pipeline from the well of Arindam to the Nursery. Janet paid for the pipe from the well to her hut and Mother gave us the funds for the remainder of the pipe for covering the area between Janet's hut and the Nursery. The Tamil men, Richard, Howard and Dirk worked long hours with picks, etc, digging the holes. Finally the plastic pipe was glued together piece by piece, laid into the ground and the water was turned on. For three days it worked beautifully, then as we were waiting for water for filling our barrels and cement rings, nothing came out. After investigating, to our dismay we discovered that eight links of the pipe had completely collapsed. After dismissing such possibilities as sabotage (we learned after the digging began that we were digging right into an ancient Tamil burial ground much to the chagrin of the local people) and melting from the sun, we surmised that when the pump was shut off the rushing back of the water had created a vacuum and ultimately we found many links of faulty pipe which had been unable to withstand the pressure that had cracked irreparably from the strain. After weeks of inconvenience and stalling from the pipe company in Madras, an air bleed valve was installed as well as a non-return valve. The pipe is now in good working condition and recently we purchased more cement rings for increased water storage. We have all begun to grow accustomed to such occurrences in Auroville, however, as it seems the simplest (sometimes the biggest as in the case of the dam at Forecomers) experiments that one would be able to undertake and complete so easily and with precision in the outside world seem to become monumental problems here. Whatever the situation may be (our position must be to refuse the attempt of the hostile forces to gain control and to continue to persevere in our work), we are given constant encouragement by the Mother, and just recently She sent us a beautiful red and white double hibiscus which She has named "Faith". We have planted many hot weather annuals such as Amaranthus, Helianthus, Rudbeckia, Zinnias, Marigolds, Four-o–clocks, Coreopsis and many others. Just recently we grew a beautiful light green zinnia never before shown to Mother. We sent a flower to Her and She named it "Spontaneous Endurance". In our Herb garden we have transplanted the Sweet Basil and it is now tall and wonderfully aromatic. We have grown very close to the plants and at times they even talk to us. One evening as I lay resting at Promesse the basil appeared before my eyes as in a vision. It was very, very unhappy and appeared to be crying. When I told Richard he said that he had also seen it. The next day we discovered that the plants had not been weeded and were being suffocated by weeds. In the course of the work we have had many such experiences. We have also much lemon grass which not only makes an excellent tea but is also a useful plant for the prevention of soil erosion. In the field between Howard's hut and Janet's hut we have started a large flower garden for gathering bouquets, etc. We have already transplanted Zinnias (Endurance) and Hollyhock (Offering) and will transplant many others when they are ready. In the same field we are building a lattice area which will be covered with creepers and vines and which will be used for providing an ideal condition for our hibiscus with filtered light from the vines. In another area of the land we are building a shade area with some propylite shading material from the U.S. as a protection for our seedlings against the monsoon winds and rain. A compost pit has also been completed. We are planting almost every day now and the number of plants which we now have in our care has quadrupled since we started the Nursery just four short months ago.

We are having many problems with the balance of nature on the land as the black ants and termites carry off all our seeds and eat into our plants, wood and almost anything else they touch. A coconut fiber basket left out at night is shrapnel by morning! The squirrels are also a great nuisance and must be kept under control, but we believe that these and all other problems will be annihilated by the new force and consciousness entering the land.

Some of the village children went out and gathered many tiny seedlings of Casuarina trees and helped us to plant them. We will set them out to be used as windbreaks when they grow to a larger size.

In March we planted many seeds of hybrid melons from America. Just when they were beginning to blossom a cow came in, unnoticed, and ate almost everything. This was before we had put up our fencing. Miraculously, though, they came up again as strong as ever and we are now enjoying a bountiful harvest. We are able to send a melon every few days to the Mother and Francoise makes juice of them for Her which She drinks in the afternoons. We also have shared them with many other Aurovilians and many friends in the Ashram, and many have also gone to Auroville prosperity. Our mango harvest was not too productive, but we shared what we had among the Nursery workers and friends, and I have made some jars of jam. The jackfruit was exceptional this season, and were given to Auroville prosperity.

The young papaya seedlings are now transplanted into pits and we have given many to Shyama and Frederick, Constance, Bob and Deborah, Dawn and Arindam and to some of the people from Aspiration who work with us. Brigitt, Jean-Christophe, Bernard and Fabienne and Christopher have come several times and Sebastian and Rafael, who are in charge of Francoise's garden at State House, have also come to help and learn. It is a great joy for us to be able to give in this way and to share with others as we believe this to be in the true spirit of Auroville.

We have also started some watermelon seeds from America and some Indian brinjal. We will plant more vegetables when cooler weather comes. The Los Angeles California group has been wonderful about sending seeds to us and in collecting valuable and interesting literature (on gardening). My Madicilias also sent vegetable seeds from the South which thrive very well here. A few weeks ago Carmen Neville and Suresh Hindocha gave us some lovely plants. The wife of the Director of the Bombay Branch of State Bank of India has also sent plants through Kishorilal.

Arindam

At the Nursery one day during a time when Richard and I were away, and only Howard and Radhakrishna were there, a goat came in and started eating the flowers. As is the practice in Auro-Orchard and elsewhere, Howard and Radhakrishna took the goat and tied it up in order to teach the young goatherd a lesson. The boy, obviously frightened by the idea that his father would scold him, went to his village and told that Richard had beaten him and stolen his goat. Unknown to us as we sat eating our lunch at Promesse, a plot was brewing in the village. The boy's father, an interpreter, and two men from the village descended upon Richard en masse when we returned to the Nursery. They were threatening to burn down Auroville and were prepared to begin with Howard's hut and go on from there. While the boy went on lying relentlessly, they ranted and raved that flowers have no purpose and that they do not have any use as they do not feed their starving people, so what did it matter that they had been eaten by the goats. After some time the boy confessed that he had fabricated the story and the thing was then settled. The Tamils are quite emotional people at times and melodramatic but tend to overcome their animosity quickly. For the most part we have an excellent relationship with the villagers and they have given us many helpful hints about and through the knowledge and experience handed down to them through the centuries.

At times the sky and the land are almost overwhelming in their beauty and often in the evenings we sit and marvel at the magnificence of the Indian sunsets. Each one is so unique and casts its own particular form and hue each evening. From the patio we can see the *Cassia fistula* (Mother calls it Imagination) tree with its yellow blossoms full and cascading one side toward the Nursery and on the other side toward the road. When the wind blows we are graced by its gentle and lovely fragrance. But the land can be as harsh as it is beautiful and winds of cyclonic proportions lifted Howard's roof off one afternoon and serious floods resulted. Cement was given by the Mother to reinforce the foundation.

We have all gone through some rough moments in the sun and heat and all have had mild sunstroke, liver problems and bouts with amoebas, but we go on joyfully amidst the difficulties knowing that Her help is always there and that the work will be accomplished through faith and love.

Very little is given for the gardens at present and our working fund remains at a mere Rs. 150 per month. Mother has approved a separate account for the Matrimandir Gardens and we believe when people become awakened to the meaning of these gardens and the deep significance that they will give to the city of Auroville and to all mankind, not only from the standpoint of aesthetic beauty but by the inner force and power that will emanate from them as they surround and embrace the Shrine of the Divine Mother, then we will be confident at the money which is necessary to finance such a project as this.

Anne Eggenberger

1971

Anne in a note to Richard Eggenberger, one year before Mother gave him the name, Narad

My Dearest Richard,

    I have just had the most wonderful dream about you which I shall record and try to send to you by Ramachandra, before I see you in the afternoon.

    You and I and some other people (I don't remember anyone in particular, although it seems that Mr. Chandler was present) were walking about what seems to have been a campus. We were standing in front of a very large structure which appeared to be that of St. Paul's School in England where Sri Aurobindo studied. (I had seen a picture of the school before going to sleep as I am again reading Life of Sri Aurobindo.) Forming a pinnacle around the top of the school were some tree tops which appeared to have no trunks or roots in the earth.

    Suddenly with a great burst of energy you said "I must get them for my teacher". With this you began to scale the wall of the school, by rope, with a pair of pruning clippers. All were aghast, but suddenly the branches began to fall and we could see you in the top pruning away.

    When we went to see the branches they were all golden and shimmering. When you came down we were all rejoicing and there was much happiness and joy in the atmosphere. You said, "Now we can transplant them in the earth".

    Afterwards we all began to walk about among the most

beautiful plants and flowers I have ever seen, but nothing I could clearly identify. The dream ended here.

I felt so good, as I woke up immediately after the dream. It seems to have been more like an experience than a dream.

With love in Their Light,
Anne

Mother's handwritten reply:

> It is not quite a dream,
> and it is a very good indication
> about the work you are doing.
>
> I hope Richard will recover soon.
> The packet enclosed is for him.
>
> With love and blessings
>
> **Mother**

During the 1970s

The Children's Gardening Class

During the 1970's I held a children's gardening class. Their ages were from 5 to 12. It was a time of great joy, for we shared so many wonderful experiences. There was one that topped them all, however. A beautiful Brahmini kite named Ankh, with his large wings, would never

Ankh miss the gardening class, for he loved to be with the children. My daughter Chali would wear a kind of beret which he would silently pluck off her head, fly into a nearby tree, begin laughing, and drop the hat to the ground. He would do this as well with the buns we would carry back to our houses. We would walk slowly home, and then suddenly there was no bun in our hand!

How the children loved him. As we gardened together he would fly from tree to tree to watch them. One day I was coming out of the house with a small piece of yellow cheese. Immediately Ankh flew down onto the trellis by the front door. I asked him if he would like some cheese, and held it out to him, He took it so gently, and then every day for weeks he would come for his piece of cheese. One day, knowing that I was in the house, he flew in and stood on the highest door waiting for his cheese.

The story could end there, but later I saw Ankh high in the sky with a dot above him. Slowly he descended, crying constantly, and then I saw his mate, hesitantly coming down. They landed together on the trellis, and I gave him his piece of cheese, which he ate; then the two of them flew off together.

The children's gardening class

How the children would jump with glee when he entered and they would speak to him. But back to the story of our classes. We would study insects, pollination of hibiscus, rooting cuttings and more, even making soap which one of the mothers said was the best laundry detergent ever! One day we studied grafting, and with a budding knife carefully in hand a five year old grafted different colours of plumeria on a dwarf stock to make a 'rainbow plumeria!

Years later when I returned and was at the Solar Kitchen giving an interview, two lovely young ladies rushed over to me and kissed me on the cheek, saying how happily they remembered the gardening class.

Dated in the 1970s

Letter from Narad to an Aurovilian concerning the Matrimandir Gardens Nursery and Matrimandir Gardens:

Regarding the plants in the Matrimandir Gardens and Nursery, we began with a palette virtually devoid of colour, not only in the Matrimandir but in Auroville as well, in the very early 1970's. When Mother gave me the charge to build the Gardens of the Matrimandir I set out in 1969 to find an area close to the Centre, Peace, where the Matrimandir would be built. I selected a spot that would offer the most protection for the thousands of seedlings and cuttings that would be introduced. There was a grove of mango trees with a bullock path bordering one side, a canyon to the rear, and fields to the north and east. I wrote to Mother telling Her that I found a good place to begin the Nursery (the same place that Amrit also chose) and asked Her Blessings, which She gave.

When we began the long work of species introduction and evaluation we kept detailed notes on the provenance of the genera and species as well as accession data and meticulous observations taken each Sunday on the performance and acclimatization and adaptation, or lack thereof, of the extraordinary wealth of plant material that we received through our seed exchange programmes with more than eighty Botanical Gardens in thirty countries. This research covered a period of approximately twelve years, and all the information was kept in my desk and in the Matrimandir Horticultural Library.

In addition to the weekly studies we made monthly visits to Madras to chart the seasonal diversity of native and introduced species at the Theosophical Society and the many public gardens where ornamental horticulture was of significance. We also made quarterly visits to Bangalore to exchange plants and collect seeds and cuttings from the Lal Bagh Gardens and other major gardens in the area. Our observations covered the following: time and length of flowering season, fruiting season, duration of deciduous state (if any), size of leaves, flowers, description of colours, growth habit and rate of growth, mature height and spread, and much more. I do not know what happened to these notes though I have asked about them on many occasions. I know that the Library was disbanded and the many hundreds of books given to various Aurovilians.

Perhaps something further may be suggested based on the inspiration Mother gave me then and now, to realise something of the power, beauty and majesty She was bringing down for the Gardens that would be as important as the Matrimandir itself. You may remember Her words to me, beginning with, "It must be a thing of great beauty…"

When I began with a small group of sincere and dedicated co-workers, I had no experience with tropical plants, much the same as our "Green Belt" foresters had no experience in building forests. Yet, the Grace that Mother showered upon us enabled us to open a little to the inner nature of plants and flowers, to begin to understand their cultural requirements in adapting to this rigorous and often harsh climate. In those early days there were no windbreaks, no microclimate save for the mango grove, no protection from goats and cattle, etc. We did whatever we could to care for the plants, and each time we planted we prayed to The Mother to give them the strength to survive the initial stress of adaptation and to grow and flower to perfection in an atmosphere charged with the Divine Grace. We prayed that we might also do the same!

Empiric observations are a valid beginning along with sound horticultural techniques, but I believe that all the horticultural knowledge we require can be found in silent communication with Nature, attentiveness to the directives given out by a species, and from this intuitive understanding and trust in Sri Aurobindo and The Mother the Matrimandir Gardens will manifest in all their beauty and significance.

Narad

Undated

Matrimandir Gardens and Nursery by Mary Helen

This has been a busy few months as winter is the time in the tropics for most planting and propagation, in addition to being the only time of the year we 'velakarais' can work all day in the sun. About 35 new trees were added to the gardens, mostly along the road leading into the Matrimandir area. Many of these seedlings have their origin in South America or Australia and all were raised in the Nursery Gardens seed exchange program. Water supply for this and some additional outlying areas is now more efficiently supplied thanks to nearly 400m of new underground pipeline, reducing the need for long stretches of plastic hose and awkward transportation by wheelbarrow.

Mary Helen with young Chali

Work around the Banyan tree was begun again by Francois to prepare for plantation of a lawn, but has since been halted due to lack of funds. Much compost is needed and it is felt that the work should proceed only when the best conditions can be provided. Matters pertaining to the development of the gardens as well as of the construction work, are regularly discussed at the weekly Matrimandir meetings. Some of the pressing, and as yet unresolved, problems of the past few months concern land use and the villagers traditionally spread their grains to dry on special plots of sun-baked earth. Several of these plots have come into the gardens area as a result of land purchase or exchange of Parambok (government) land and have been "reclaimed", conservationally speaking, by Auroville making them unsuitable for drying the grain. Alternatively, the villagers have begun using the smooth, sunny brick rim of the amphitheater for this purpose, bringing their bullocks and bullock carts, cows and often whole families to camp there until the grains are dry, a situation regarded as being anywhere from undesirable to intolerable by Aurovilians living and working in the area. It is hoped that as Parambok land is involved the local governmental departments will collaborate in finding a solution before the next harvest season.

In the Nursery, special effort has gone into improving three particular plant groups: Plumerias, Hibiscus and Orchids. Many of the Plumeria (Psychological Perfection) cuttings brought back 2½ years ago from Hawaii and Singapore have been planted out and are beginning to flower, and new cuttings were received from Waimea Arboretum in Hawaii bringing the collection to around 75 different varieties. A number of new Hibiscus plants and cuttings were obtained from the Lal Bagh Botanical Garden in Bangalore when Narad and Bill Imig made a trip there last month. With these plants – which represent some of the original and best hybridization work done in India – and other special hybrids given to Auroville by the American Hibiscus Society, a good basis is formed for Bill's beginning experiments in hybridizing. He has also continued to improve cultural methods; one successful experiment has been mulching with shredded coconut fibre, a material that is cheap, easily available, moisture retentive and has a soft, neat appearance.

The Orchid population has exploded recently thanks to generous gifts totaling about 2,500 plants, including around 100 completely new species or hybrids. Aurovilians on trips to Germany brought back several special varieties, a contribution made possible by a careful selection from a grower in Thailand, and a trip by Narad and Mary Helen to Sri Lanka brought many beautiful and valuable additions as well as contacts with breeders, new tips on culture and information on how to set up a simple laboratory for seed propagation. Any future hybridization will be greatly enriched by an impressive five volume set of books just received from Matagiri in the U.S. containing the names and parentage of all the registered orchids in the world (there are about 30,000 naturally occurring species and about 100,000 man-made hybrids!).

Eric Hughes of Matagiri, one of the most helpful people for the gardens

Miscellaneous news includes bunding, contouring and planting of windbreaks and several species of Cassia and Plumeria in the new fields; the new pump and well are functioning at last and the first section of pipeline has been installed; a new lamb adds another mouth to the family of woolly lawn–mowers; a gratefully received donation enabled the purchase of much needed tires for both bullock carts; John Harper has just completed a new solar heater donated by a regular visitor to Auroville, Rutledge Tompkins; and preparations are underway for the second flower show to be held this year on Auroville's twelfth birthday, February 28 and 29 (the first was last year on the Mother's birthday, February 21).

Admiral Rutledge Tompkins

[*Second part of the newsletter dated April 1970, written to friends by Richard and Anie Eggenberger; the first part of which we reproduced in this document on the date 18th December 1969 and the third part on the date April 1970:*]

On January 17th we brought a new force of Work to the Center which had fallen somewhat into a state of inertia and neglect. We began weeding, grading and leveling the area around the rock garden, grading the embankment and filling in the holes created through erosion during the monsoon.

Between that time and the February 28th celebration, we planted approximately 10,000 cuttings of "Sri Aurobindo's Compassion" (Portulaca) which are thriving beautifully but must be watered every day by hand, as there is no other method for supplying water to that area at the moment.

One evening, before a UNESCO official was due to arrive, Richard was told that the amphitheatre must be graded and leveled by the next morning at 10.00am. So he and a crew of workers worked an all-night shift to prepare the theatre for her visit. The section around the urn was painted an earth color and the amphitheatre was completed. The result was an overnight miracle. For February 28th we secured around 60 potted plants which were arranged free-form around the banyan tree. There was joy that day. Afterwards they were moved to the Nursery which we set up just prior to the 28th. Also during this time the Geological Survey of India was at the Center for about 3 weeks boring a well at a site designated by Mother. Each day Richard made about twelve trips by tractor to the well at "Arindam" supplying them with barrels of water, as they used a type of pressed mud to bore the well. The project was completed and water was struck at a depth of 500ft yielding about 5,000 gallons per hour. We await the installation of electricity at the center as this pump will be generated by electrical power.

Narad and Anie

3rd April, 1970

[*Third part of the newsletter written to friends by Richard and Anie Eggenberger, the first part of which we produced dated December 1969 and the second dated January 1970:*]

For about five weeks our greatest concentration of energy has gone into the Nursery: building wooden flats, three-tiered shelves for holding pots and flats, mixing soils, painting with coal tar to protect against ants, termites and other pests with which we are constantly plagued. We have planted banana trees, hybrid melons, papaya seeds (65% germinated), cherimoya seeds, titonia, marigold and an herb garden of basil, chives and dill. We are unable to plant anything more as the water situation is unresolved at present. Our only source of water has been two small barrels a day brought in by bullock cart. All of the above mentioned plants, seeds, seedlings, etc, must be watered daily by hand, which is a time consuming and strenuous job. However, we are at the moment digging a pipeline from the well at "Arindam" to Janet's hut and on to the Nursery. We also conducted an experiment of composting and mulching the mango trees on the land with straw mulch. Trenches of about 18in depth were dug around the trees and the mulch filled in. The area was heavily watered and the trees have gone for one month without water and have not dried out. The trees absorb the existing moisture as is needed. Soil tests were also given by the Government of India and the report revealed that the soil is almost completely depleted of every nutrient.

At the Nursery site Richard has designed a lovely patio of native red brick surrounded by many graceful, cool ferns. Comfortable seating has been arranged as we want people to be able to sit and relax and absorb the atmosphere and the powers emanating from the plants and flowers and trees. As is always the situation, our work force in the first few days was good. However, due to hard work, many have dropped away - and for many weeks the work was done solely by Richard, myself and Howard Iriyama, a Japanese-American boy. Howard has a natural love and feel for the plants and has worked steadily throughout with an inspiring, selfless devotion. He has never refused to do any of the most strenuous of tasks, and has done on many occasions the work which would normally require two men. Mother gave him blessings to live at the Nursery site. He took the foundation of a hut that belonged to Constance and with some help he has constructed one of the most beautiful huts in all of Auroville. There is such a feeling of peace, beauty and simplicity. We have had some bad encounters along the way with village people and their goats, but for the most part they have at times joined in the work with a real spontaneous joy. We have tried not to hire anyone, but would rather do the work ourselves as Mother has requested. At present we now have with us a Dutch boy named Dirk and an extraordinary Tamil boy named Radhakrishna. He is an extremely refined and intelligent boy and is one of the few who is working there according to the Auroville system. He receives no pay and works from early morning to late evening. Richard has taught him to drive the tractor and we are helping him to learn English. He takes his lunch with us and we teach him what we can. In the beginning we sent a letter to the Mother asking if we should send names of those wishing to work with us for Her permission. Her answer was "If people are sincerely wanting to work in harmony and collaboration, there is no need of asking my permission."

The Mother has granted us a small monthly working fund which, due to our constant expansion, will not continue to serve us too much longer. There are many needs which are absolutely essential for this work in order to realize her vision and to bring it into full manifestation. We are very grateful for the interest you have shown.

14 January 1972

Meeting with Mother

Received Darshan of the Mother, together with Neil and Huta, for the work of the Savitri slides and music. I gave Mother the following flowers:
- Seeking for All Support in the Divine
- To Live Only for the Divine

- Aspiration for Vital Purity
- Aspiration for Silence in the Mind
- Radiating Vital Purity
- Renunciation of Vital Desires
- Humility in the Love for the Divine
- Light in the Vital Movements

Mother looked very deeply into me three times during the Darshan. She also asked how many slides there were, touched the slides, and said… "Magnificent". She then wrote Her Blessings on a large photo card and gave one to Neil and one to me.

15 February 1972

Visit to Mother in company with Richard Pearson

Richard Pearson and I went to Mother with paintings, line drawings, flowers and the manuscript of the book. Richard entered first and knelt at Mother's side. I knelt in front of Mother.

She made a joke in French about the two Richards and pulled at Her chin as if humorously identifying me by my beard. Then She said a joyous 'Bonjour' to me.

After presenting all the parts of the book I gave Mother a dark purple Sinningia and She said "magnificent" twice, and was truly thrilled with its beauty. I had also presented Mother earlier with two large Hawaiian Hibiscus, 'Power of the Supramental Consciousness' and 'Sweetness of the Power Surrendered to the Divine'.

Narad (centre) with Richard Pearson (left)

Then Mother asked about all the flowers as to whether they had been given a significance and Richard told Her. I then gave Mother a cream-white Abutilon and an Echinacea from the Matrimandir Gardens Nursery. She touched the Abutilon all over.

19 February 1972

Blessing Packet from Mother

Today I received a Blessings Packet from Mother for the beginning of the third year of the Matrimandir Gardens Nursery. I also wrote Mother about the Tamil men beginning to learn something of the work. Mother replied, "They can learn the work and, if careful, do it."

21 February 1972

Mother's birthday

Howard (Amrit) and I sent flowers to Mother on Her birthday. Some of the flowers were 'Receptivity',
'Vital Consecration',
'Integral Attachment to the Divine',
'To Live Only for the Divine',
'Aristocracy' and others.

Mother sent us each a Blessing Packet through Shyamsundar. At six in the morning we gathered together and placed stones in the cement mixer for the first pillar of the Matrimandir.

Nolini read a message from the Mother and we listened to Mother reciting "The Hour of God". I had an intense experience and wept. Mother later said that She felt like it was everyone's birthday and that something manifested.

28 July 1972

Visit to Mother

I went to Mother today about 11:45. Mother does not see people on Saturday so I was given today.

As I entered my name was called out, Richard Eggenberger. Champaklal showed me where to kneel. I knelt and offered myself to Mother, tried to pour everything at Her Feet. She looked at me for some time, a look unlike anything I had ever seen before, as if She was looking at another person and didn't see Richard any longer.

She gave me a card and bouquet while looking at me, then said, "Look at your card". I put the flowers down and opened the card. Mother had given me a new name! She had written below my old name and above the new one, Narad! I was overcome with joy and gratitude and filled with tears. I put my head on Mother's Feet and stayed there for a while, weeping.

When I rose She looked at me again, placed Her hand firmly on my head and looked some more and smiled – and it was my time to leave Her.

1973

Extracts from the diary of a visitor

I was persuaded to join in concreting a support pillar for the Matrimandir, sitting on a crossbeam passing metal dishes of concrete mix to the next man in line. While I was doing this my wife worked in the kitchen of the Matrimandir Worker's Camp, also known as Centre Kitchen, helping to prepare lunch for everybody.

* * *

I helped Patricia and a man named Alan swap houses over a distance of some 400m. There was an interesting background to the swap, because Patricia had wanted for some time to find a quieter place, but wasn't sure it was best for her. She had prayed to Mother for guidance, and 30 minutes later Alan had appeared and asked if she was interested in a swap! Coincidence?

* * *

After lunch we went down to the Nursery and swept up leaves, then went over to the Matrimandir site to help with a concreting. On finishing, we had to have a bucket wash as there was no water in Centre Camp, thanks to the pump being rendered inoperative by a power cut, which was happening up to 18 hours a day at the time.

* * *

We were very much enjoying the company of people like Roger & Patricia, Tom & Maggie, Angela, Narad & Mary Helen – mother to the children's friend Chali – but I knew that it was not enough to come for people alone, and one had to be equally drawn to participate in the project of Auroville regardless of the human factor.

* * *

I am not especially sensitive, but I immediately noticed a strong and beautiful atmosphere inside Mother's room. I suppose it was all the talk we had absorbed about her which affected my impression, but I had the distinct feeling of being in the presence of someone extraordinary, someone more than just an ordinary human being.

My wife went first to Mother, getting her Blessing Packet. Then it was my turn. I was in a daze, but I knelt with head bowed, resting my forehead on the material of Mother's garments on the left edge of her chair. As I did so, I felt Mother's hand gently touch my head, then assuming that was 'IT', I took the proferred silvery Blessing Packet from her, stood up, and started towards the door. I had taken one or two paces, when something made me look again at Mother, and I saw that she had turned her head as though to follow me with her eyes as I moved away. That is the moment when I feel a bond with her was made, because earlier I hadn't looked into her eyes, as everyone else apparently did.

Then it was over, and with my eyes wet with emotion I was at the door and going down the stairs to the courtyard, feeling in a state of utter peace, and conscious of nothing but a surging aspiration to improve myself and be worthy of Mother and what she had given me.

* * *

We visited Shyamsundar, sitting cross legged on a plain chair behind his desk at the Beach Office, and got an OK to stay in a hut in the Nursery – subject to complying with the accepted rules for the area, which were to do work and to live cleanly without drugs, sex or alcohol.

* * *

I worked for three hours in the full sun, but then had to give up, completely dehydrated and with a slight headache. Looking back it was pretty stupid of me, as the Indian sun is as fierce as you can find anywhere on earth, and I should have confined my efforts to the early morning or late afternoon.

I did a bit more work in the afternoon, then set up hoses to water some young Frangipani trees, though I couldn't start the watering until the electricity came back on at 6.45pm. Since dinner was at seven, this obliged me to water in the dark, a problem compounded by the fact that the pressure was so great that the hose connections kept blowing open, and I had to go to the pump house several hundred metres away each time and turn off the pump to effect a join, then return again to start the pump. After doing this twice, I gave up. On going to bed I set the alarm for 3.00am to do the last night-watch at Matrimandir.

* * *

After breakfast I weeded around the rose pots, then in the afternoon went to Pondy to search for cow dung compost for Narad (Rs.50 a lorryload), and drive belts for the water pump.

* * *

One interesting person not mentioned is the "Amma" of the banyan tree (take the photo of her in *"A family odyssey"*), a local village woman who occupies a small primitive hut between the tree and the Matrimandir construction site. We are told she has been there since 1966, and has been accepted as an Aurovilian. Most days and evenings she can be found sitting by the tree, ever friendly and smiling. The contrast between her ultra-simple village-style hut and the complexity of the Matrimandir now arising beside it seems extreme.

* * *

Our two children (left and right) with Chali (centre) - three happy ragamuffins!

We were finding the work very satisfying, but also very hard and demanding. Meanwhile I was determined to try and get the rose collection in tip-top shape before we left.

* * *

During the night I had to get up at 3.15am to switch off the pump, which I would have preferred to avoid but had accepted to do for Narad. He ran the Nursery in a somewhat Western managerial style, though with great efficiency and wonderful results. Mother herself had encouraged him to take up the work, and he had developed an excellent memory for the hundreds of plant names she had given based on their psychic significance. At the time he was doing a lot of research into indigenous species of trees and shrubs, and was constantly noting down their characteristics – their flowering and seeding times, their water needs, their placement in relation to sun and shade and other plants, etc. We had great respect for him, so were happy to do what we could in support. I especially noted his voice, so unique that I could have recognized it in a crowd anywhere in the world.

* * *

My wife had found a very meaningful passage in the writings of Sri Aurobindo, as follows:

"What you feel about physical things is true – there is a consciousness in them, a life which is not the life and consciousness of man and animal which we know, but still secret and real. That is why we must have respect for physical things and use them rightly, not misuse and waste, ill-treat or handle them with a careless roughness."

* * *

After dinner, in company with Narad and Alan I helped with filling tanks and watering in the Nursery, which again had been impossible during the day because of the massive power cuts we were still experiencing. We finished late, having done everything except fill the main tank, but I then had to get up again at 2.30am to switch the pump off. Walking back from the pump house I couldn't help feeling that garden work in Auroville at this time was a virtual 24-hour affair!

* * *

I was reading a book in the morning, and came across a fascinating story which gave me a fresh insight into the consciousness of plants and trees. Apparently Mother had received a "call" from the central banyan tree in Auroville, and had sent a man up from Pondy to investigate. When he returned, he reported to Mother that he had at first not seen anything unusual, but had then spotted a machete (cutty in local parlance) embedded in the trunk, and had removed it. Mother then informed him that she already knew this through her inner contact with the tree!

* * *

During the morning two men arrived in a Jeep from the Auroville Office in Pondy bearing a chit, and went over to Tom & Maggie's house demanding five jackfruit. According to Maggie they were rather unpleasant and rude in their demands, and a nasty row ensued, at the end of which Maggie told them she wouldn't give any fruit. The men then returned to Pondy, saying that they intended to report the matter to Shyamsundar and return after lunch for the fruit.

After lunch Maggie was resting inside her house, when she heard heavy thudding noises outside. She ran out, and found SIX jackfruit had fallen from the tree and were lying on the ground. They hadn't been cut down or their stems chewed, they had simply fallen, and six at the same time! Botanically it was impossible, because jackfruit don't fall, they have to be harvested one by one from the tree, but it had happened. Maggie felt shattered, wondering if it was a personal lesson for her?

Of the many coincidental and unusual things to happen during our seven weeks stay in Auroville, this was for us the most extraordinary, and no-one ever came up with an explanation. I did, however, feel that there was a lesson in it for the people of Auroville.

Approx 1974

Excerpt from the book "Auroville, the First Six Years" by Savitra

[Savitra's account of the beginnings of the Matrimandir Nursery:]

To begin the preparation for developing Matrimandir Gardens a Nursery was begun on February 21st 1970, behind the site where the workers camp would rise in the following year. The work would be overseen by Narad, who had received 10 years training in temperate horticulture and 2 years in sub tropical horticulture before his five years experience in Auroville.

* * *

This particular site was chosen because it was the one on a plot with trees (i.e. mango and jackfruit trees) in the area. Narad's "experience in Auroville" started at the end of 1969.

2 March 1976

Note written by C.N.Sundaram of the Government of Tamil Nadu, Forest Department, following his visit to the Matrimandir Gardens

1. On 2.3.1976 morning along with Mr. Mohammed Zackriah the District Forest Officer of Cuddalore Division I reached Matrimandir Gardens by 10.00am. This garden is very close to Matrimandir which is the geographical as well as the spiritual centre of Auroville and extends over an area of 7 acres. Mr. Narad, the architect of this garden over the last 7 years, was all smiles and courtesy to receive us and show us round. He is a landscape designer by profession.
2. The land before he took up the work in 1968 was barren. The soil is not too good and it is mostly red clay with a good admixture of pebbles. Water has to come to this area from a well which is 1,000 feet away. With great perseverance and determination he has turned this land into a marvel of trees, flowers, shrubs and cover crops.
3. He has 75 varieties of Bougainvilleas, 25 varieties of plumerias, 100 varieties of Hibiscus, 22 varieties of

Bauhinias, 4 varieties of Michelins, 7 varieties of Nerium, 5 varieties of Tabebuias, many varieties of Acacias, Peltophorums, Poincianas, Catesbaea espinosa, Alstonias, Cochlospermums, Lagerstroemias and many varieties of Cannas, Ipomoeas, Jasmine and Zephyranthes XH indigenous as well as exotics from the U.S., Australia and a few other countries.

4. He has a bamboo clump of Alphonse carr,, a few trees of Peltaphorum vogelianum, Peltaphorum pterocarpum and Peltaphorum africanum, a tree of Milletia ovalifolia with lavender flowers, Guaiacum official with blue flowers, three varieties of Bixa orellana, the seeds of which are used to colour butter and cheese throughout the world. All told nearly 1,000 species of flowering trees and plants all in 7 acres.

5. He has a glass house where he has some varieties of orchids from U.S.A. and Australia, and one flower on a Phalaenopsis orchid is still fresh even after 40 days! He is trying out some Avocado (Butter fruit) plants here.

6. He has also a seed store where seeds of nearly 250 varieties in the Auroville area are available for anyone who wishes to plant and care for them. However, the seed store is mainly for the exchange of seeds with Botanical Gardens and Arboreta throughout the world.

7. He is also interested himself in the manufacture of "Ornamental planters" (pots) of fairly big sizes with Rajasthan marble studded over reinforced concrete pots which are really very attractive.

8. This complex Nursery project which has the Blessings of Mother of Sri Aurobindo Ashram, Pondicherry, was started as a nucleus to afforest Auroville, by forming a

Green Belt on the periphery so as to create a micro-climate in the city which will be located in the centre of the belt. The Mother has said about this, "It must be a thing of great beauty, of such a beauty that when men enter they will say, 'Ah, this is it' and will experience physically and concretely the experience of each garden. In the garden of Youth, they will know youth, etc. One must know how to move from consciousnesss to consciousness". (These were the Mother's own words to Mr. Narad and they are the guiding light of his life and work here.) He has to build the twelve gardens of theMatrimandir with another garden, the Garden of Unity, which will surround the Banyan tree, and they must be the most beautiful gardens the earth has ever seen.
9. In the project his work is ably shared by Mr. Alan in the glass house and seed storage programme, and Miss Mary Helen in flowering plants. She does some Bonsai work too.
10. The place is worth a visit or more by Foresters, Agriculturists and all lovers of Trees, Plants and Flowers.

1977

Auroville is a Door

Auroville is a door opening on a truer vision of Life. Those who are touched by this truth are as men standing on the threshold looking out on their souls.

Auroville is the meeting place of the earth's call for perfection and the Divine's response.

Auroville, innocent and naïve, holds the power for the world's perfection but needs to be in harmony with the wisdom of India to effectuate in collaboration with all people, in Sri Aurobindo's words, "the great and difficult thing which is the aim of our endeavour".

Narad

early April 1978

An incident at nearby Bharat Nivas

It was a very difficult time for Auroville, when competing entities were attempting to take control of the budding township. One day a young girl came running to the Matrimandir Gardens Nursery, tears flowing from her face, and said, "The gundas at Bharat Nivas are beating Frederick and David to death. Please help." It seems that the Sri Aurobindo Society had hired a large number of thugs incase of problems at Bharat Nivas, which at the time was a building site and their headquarters in Auroville. Frederick and David were there trying to find a way of taking it over.

All the workers at the Nursery gathered around me and we left to see if we could save these two courageous souls. I picked up a machete and we left the Nursery to go to the road. Immediately a Voice from above said clearly and strongly to me, "Drop the Weapon". I dropped it immediately, and then from deep within I began to say "Ma, Ma" in my strongest voice.

You would find it hard to believe what happened next. These thugs parted like the Red Sea and I walked through them, put David on my shoulder and carried him out, all the while chanting "Ma, Ma". When I reach B (Bill), I stopped chanting Ma as I handed David over to him. At that moment a rock was thrown by one of the thugs and my head was split open. I was immediately taken to the main Government hospital in Pondicherry, where the wound was cleansed and stitched. Afterwards Mary Helen took me to see Nolini, who turned almost white on seeing the large bandages and gave me his blessing.

July / August 1978

Matrimandir Gardens by Richard M. Eggenberger

This is written partly in reply to Mr. Eric Golby's brief but excellent report on Mr. Sharma's hybridizing work in Bangalore. It is also an opportunity for me to share with the members of the American Hibiscus Society something of the work we have been doing at the Matrimandir Gardens in Auroville during the past seven years.

Auroville was inaugurated on February 28, 1968. The soil from 124 nations was deposited in an urn at the centre of the future city by two children from each country, a symbolic beginning to the city that aspires to be a model of human unity. Presently, about 400 people from many parts of the world are working together on the initial stages of the city's development.

At the centre of the city is the Matrimandir. As in some of the great cities of the past where a temple or a church was the focal point, the starting point in the construction of the city, so too the Matrimandir is the beginning and the essence of Auroville. It is the unifying force of our life and work. Now well on its way to completion, built entirely by an international crew of unskilled workers, it is said to be one of the most perfect structures. Its form is that of a compressed sphere symbolizing perhaps a sun rising from the earth. The outer 'skin' of the Matrimandir may be covered by solar collectors. The study of this possibility will be undertaken at the University of Arizona under the guidance and inspiration of Dr. Jeffrey Cook. The central room of the structure will have walls of pure white marble which has just arrived from Italy. The entire room will be empty except for a carpet and a single ray of light which will fall on a crystal globe set over the symbols of the founders whose vision of the unity of all mankind has made possible this first experiment towards the realisation.

Ten of the twelve Gardens that will surround the Matrimandir will be represented by hibiscus. The two remaining Gardens will be represented by water-lilies and cacti and plumeria varieties.

For the first time in seven years of developing the Matrimandir Gardens I had the opportunity to visit, together with my colleague Mary Helen, some of the finest botanic gardens of the world during a spring and summer tour last year. Everywhere people spontaneously offered their assistance in innumerable ways. Directors of many gardens personally met with us and offered seeds and plants of beautiful and rare species. Many of these are now establishing well in our seven acre nursery.

Hibiscus in India

One of our most important visits was a three week tour of Florida where we had an opportunity to meet many wonderful and generous people. In the orchid world we met the entire Fennell family, Mr. & Mrs. Lewis Vaughn, Mr. Jean Merkel, Mr. Joe Samuels and some of his colleagues of the Miami Beach Parks Department who gave us a thorough tour of all the parks and public areas in their care. Mr. Bob Kundtz, Vice President and Horticultural Director of Cypress Gardens, personally showed us the entire gardens including his nursery of rare plants from all parts of the world. Mr. Perry Slocum gave us a tour of his water gardens and growing grounds and today we have many of his water-lilies at our nursery. Mr. Tony Virginia, Horticulturist at Disney World, shared his knowledge and experience of growing conditions both at Disneyland and Disney World and gave us numerous suggestions for ground covers, grasses and

ornamental plants for the tropics. We studied the landscaping and flora of the Sunken Gardens at St. Petersburg, and visited many

other gardens, including the excellent Marie Selby Botanic Gardens.

One of our most memorable days was May 23 when we met in succession three of the men most responsible for creating the beauty of

the present day hibiscus hybrids and bringing an increased public awareness and appreciation of the magnificence of this genera. Our first meeting was with Mr. Eric Golby at Reasoner's Nursery. Mr. Golby took time out from a day of rest to take us around Reasoner's and show us many of the extraordinarily beautiful hybrids available today. He generously shared with us his knowledge of breeding techniques and gave us many insights into the evolution of various species. He recommended that we visit Ross Gast's Evolutionary Garden at Waimea, Hawaii (which we did), and suggested that we visit Mr. Harry Goulding and Mr. & Mrs. Gordon Fore. On leaving he presented us with a copy of *What Every Hibiscus Grower Should Know*.

Our visit with Mr. Goulding was unforgettable. I can only add my small mite of praise to the vast encomium that has already been bestowed on this cheerful and unpretentious man. In our study of water-lilies, we found that Dr. George Pring at the Missouri Botanic Garden in St. Louis kept detailed records of all his work with tropicals, but Marliac in France kept his work on the hardy lilies a closely guarded secret, and all his years of experimentation and success are lost to the world. Mr. Goulding shared everything. He even gave to me his styrofoam hat as a parting gift! In a simple and lucid style he conveyed as much as we could absorb, with Mary Helen taking detailed notes on every aspect of breeding, culture and care. The love and attention he brings to his work was evident in all he showed us. We received from him the basics of sound hibiscus culture.

Our last meeting of the day was a visit and cordial welcome by Mr. and Mrs. Fore. Mr. Fore showed us his hibiscus collection and gave us a step-by-step demonstration of his grafting methods, which we photographed on slides and have studied often here in Auroville. We became members of the Society that evening. Since joining the Society, we have received a packet of 100 seeds of 18 crosses by three different breeders. As Mrs. Shepard cautioned us, the seeds were old and only 13 of the 100 germinated. However, we have with us today some robust seedlings of Twinkle Star x Ala Moana Beauty, Ritt 424 x Kinchen's Yellow, Honolulu Lani x Evening Sunset, Ross Estey x Edith Veland, Confetti x Betsy, and Geisha Girl x All Aglow, and we're ready to fulfill Mr. Golby's wish that some of the most beautiful of the Florida hibiscus might come to India to help in our breeding work.

This summer, one of our colleagues, Alan Klass, who is in charge of the orchid collection at the Matrimandir Gardens, will make a trip to Florida to visit his

Alan Klass (left) with Narad and Mary Helen

family and study orchids. He will carry with him the proper import permits from the Government of India to bring back as many of the most beautiful orchids possible, and we would all be most grateful for any hibiscus hybrids that could be spared by members of the A.H.S. which he could carry back with him as well.

Our life and work is on the other side of the earth, but we are close to all who love hibiscus, work to inspire this love in others, and aim for perfection in breeding and culture.

12 August 1980

Letter from The Chief Conservator of Forests, K.A. Bhoja Shetty, I.F.S., to Thiru Kondas, IFS, State Silviculturist, Forest Department, Government of Tamil Nadu

My Dear Kondas,

Sub. Supply of seeds to Matrimandir Gardens, Auroville.

Mr. Richard Eggenberger (Narad), Matrimandir Gardens, requires about I kg. Gyrocarpus jacquini seeds. I request you to arrange the supply free of charge since the seeds are required for experimental purposes.

Matrimandir Gardens are a paradise for botanists and tree lovers and it is indeed an unforgettable experience to visit this place. Mr. Eggenberger and his colleagues are very helpful and will give all the information regarding the plants introduced. You may be able to get seeds from them for your trials in research gardens.

Yours sincerely,
K.A. Bhoja Shetty

11th February 1981

Letter from S.Kondas, I.F.S., Conservator of Forests (Research), Tamil Nadu.

Dear Narad,

Thank you for your letter, dated 9.2.1981.

When I visited Matrimandir Gardens last time I was impressed with the varieties of plant
species obtained from different places in the world and assembled in the Gardens. But I
unfortunately missed you. However, Mr. Daniel and other colleagues of yours have given
information regarding the creation of this beautiful Garden.

I am seriously thinking of visiting the Gardens again; perhaps in the first week of March,
'81. I hope to see you at that time as I have some ideas to share with you.

Kindly let me know whether you will be in the Gardens during the first week of March '81
so that I can confirm my tour programmes.

Yours sincerely,
Signed
(S. Kondas)

Undated

Report on the Matrimandir Gardens

[The following is from a report prepared by Narad and other Matrimandir

Gardens workers on the development of the Gardens and the Nursery from inception to date.]

Initial phase 1970-77

To begin this report and establish our research on a higher basis we must look to the words of the Mother and know something of Her relationship with plants and flowers. She speaks of the vegetal kingdom: "Have you ever watched a forest with all its countless trees and plants struggling to catch the light - twisting and trying in a hundred ways to be in the sun? That is precisely the feeling of aspiration in the physical - the urge, the movement, the push towards the light. Plants have more of it in their physical being than man. Their whole life is a worship of light. Light is, of course, the material symbol of the Divine, and the sun represents, under material conditions, the supreme Consciousness. The plants feel it quite distinctly in their own simple, blind way. Their aspiration is intense, if you know how to become aware of it". And again, of the movement of love in plants: "The movement of love is not limited to human beings and it is perhaps less distorted in worlds other than

the human world. Look at the flowers and trees. When the sun sets and all becomes silent, sit down for a moment and put yourself into communion with Nature. You will feel, rising from the earth, from below, the roots of the trees, and mounting upward and coursing through their fibres, up to the highest outstretching branches, the aspiration of an intense love and longing - a longing for something that brings light and gives happiness - for the light that is gone and they wish to have back again. There is a yearning so pure and intense that if you can feel the movement in the trees, your own being too will go up in an ardent prayer for the peace and light and love that are unmanifested here". These and many other illuminating statements are found in the book 'Flowers and Their Messages', which can serve as the starting point for our understanding of the significance of flowers and their relationship to man.

The work of building the Matrimandir Gardens will also proceed in this way, as in time we will see that "the whole creation will become more conscious; thus the vegetal kingdom will participate in its progress in accordance with its own nature". This initial participation can be felt even now, and at times witnessed. I have personally experienced the calm and protectiveness of a certain tree and its vibrations of healing. I have heard the call of another
tree directing me to look at its first flower, a single blossom of ethereal blue. I have seen a species come into flower within a year, when every reference work in our library stated that it would take 8 years or more! Certainly the vibrations of the flowers often penetrate through to our inner selves, awakening joy and aspiration, deepening peace and calm.

Possibly greater in importance than all the technical research will be the study of the messages of the flowers and the ways in which they are helping us to rise beyond the narrow limits of self, in the words of the Mother: "Perhaps the beauty of flowers too is a means used by Nature to awaken in human beings the attraction for the psychic".

These reports are, to me, the record of the birth of a garden and its infancy. There are numerous lists of scientific

names and data detailing the research completed to date. There is, however, another aspect, one that bears a mostly unspoken testimony to the collective growth and aspiration of Aurovilians from all parts of the world, whether they live with us permanently or have come to offer their energies for a few weeks or a few months, and that the love
and the will they bring to build the Matrimandir, the soul of Auroville, in this dawn of the golden age. The Mother has written: "The Matrimandir will be the soul of Auroville. The sooner the soul is there, the better it will be for everybody and especially for the Aurovilians".

In this report I should like to place in a clear perspective the major areas in which I feel the Matrimandir Gardens and subsequently all of Auroville can become a prototype of a consciously developed, balanced ecology. We can also manifest a living proof of the true harmony possible between man and his environment. A collaboration between concerned individuals and a sympathetic government aware of the need of returning the Motherland to health and fertility can be achieved by the sincere efforts of men of goodwill.

History of the Matrimandir Nursery and Gardens

Preparation for the future Gardens began with the formation of a Nursery on February 21, 1970. The site, located in a mango grove a few hundred yards west of the Banyan tree at the centre of the city, was chosen because it provided the only shade and protection in the surrounding area. Among the first things planted in the Nursery were thousands of seeds brought from California.

In the beginning four Aurovilians began working with a budget of $20 per month, clearing the land, establishing a water supply, gathering the simple tools locally available, developing a working relationship with Tamil people living in the area, and learning about a completely new world of plants in the tropics. Though our present budget is nearly $150 a month, just enough for the basic requirements of daily maintenance, the conditions which challenged the workers in the first years are still facing us today. The expansion and refinement which have taken place during the past years to enable us to meet and overcome these conditions has come in many ways: by the donation of funds and equipment, and by friends of Auroville in India and abroad and through the skills, energy, knowledge and goodwill of people who have been with us here, whether for several days or several years.

As recently as 100 years ago the broad area of coastline on which Auroville is situated was covered with dense tropical forests. Since the removal of these forests the land has suffered severe erosion of the topsoil, and in areas where the topsoil remains it has been depleted of nutrients due to uncontrolled and excessive grazing and to a lack of knowledge of crop rotation, soil conservation and rebuilding methods. Over most of the area of the Nursery, the surface is now red clay, which bakes hard in dry weather and becomes a quagmire in the rainy season. Wherever a plant is put into the ground, whether a tree or an annual, a large pit or bed must be dug, the red clay removed and replaced with a mixture of topsoil hauled in by bullock cart, and compost made by the slow accumulation and breaking down of leaves and other cuttings. The dense and always hungry populations of insects and rodents quickly developed a taste for the new, foreign species of plants being introduced, as did the domestic but equally hungry herds of cows and goats which roam freely from the villages. In an effort to avoid adding chemicals to the already damaged ecological balance, we try to control insects either by hand or by other, natural means. Cows and goats are somewhat easier as they can be guarded against by the erection of temporary thorn fences.

Initially one of the major projects was to lay a pipeline from a well 1,000 feet away to storage tanks in the Nursery. Through the years this water system has been gradually refined and expanded so that it now includes two large storage tanks containing about 10,000 gallons and 4 sets of cement rings which store enough water above the ground to take care of the most critical watering needs by gravity during the frequent electricity failures. During the dry, hot season the pump at the well site must be kept running 20 hours a day in order to maintain the Nursery. Since it is at this time of the year that we are affected by the widespread electricity shortages and cuts, we have had to purchase a diesel pump as an auxiliary at the well, and a kerosene pump as an alternative to the small electric pump at the storage tanks within the Nursery. Water from these tanks is dispersed throughout the Nursery by an underground pipe system designed by visitors from Holland and England. From these outlets the plants are watered by plastic hoses held together, since
Indian hoses have no couplings, by wire and the persistence of the young Tamil boys who work with us. Makeshift though this system may be, it is remarkably efficient, and has somehow sufficed to serve our expanding needs for the

past 6 years. Now, however, we have reached the maximum capacity for our shallow well; to date the single well is serving several thousand plants on 6 acres.

When the attempt was made in the first year to introduce seeds brought from California, it was not realised that the work of collecting and introducing new species would become the most extensive work of the Nursery. Efforts were first made to locate and visit places in India where there were established collections of plants, mostly botanic gardens originally planted by British horticulturists and botanists. The work done by these men is admirable and of invaluable use to us as we were able to see mature living examples of things described in the excellent books done by the indefatigable British botanists. The problem now became one of nomenclature and identification since, after the departure of the original collectors, the botanic gardens have suffered from a bureaucracy that has put them under the direction of men chosen for their government positions rather than their botanical knowledge. We soon realised that we would have to find more accurate sources of information, and began collecting books that were to be the beginning of our growing library. Gradually, through trips to Bangalore, Delhi, Calcutta and other places, plants already introduced or indigenous to India were identified and brought to the Nursery for study. As long as space was available, one plant of each new species was put into the ground under the best possible growing conditions, and weekly observations were made to record the growth, health, and characteristics of flowering, foliage, fruits, etc. For 3 years this information on young plants was augmented by monthly trips to several gardens in Madras and seasonal trips to Bangalore, where similar information is now being collected and entered on reference cards which will be kept in the library.

Beginning in January 1976, the work of collecting species from abroad took a great leap forward as a result of a letter sent for us by Matagiri to more than 300 botanic gardens and arboreta around the world, giving a short introduction to Auroville and our work with plants, and including our Index Seminum, which lists seeds of more than 250 species growing here, many indigenous to India. This seed exchange offer brought surprising responses from such countries as Sweden and Russia as well as tropical countries. Active correspondence has developed as a result with gardens in Australia, Hawaii, New Zealand, Africa, and several points in America, to name only a few. As we began receiving many rare species it became apparent that we needed to have more controlled conditions in which to cultivate and observe the results of the new introductions, and a small glass house was built. At about the same time a couple of orchid plants were acquired and also took up residence in the glass house. Since that time it seems that orchids have been showered upon us in monsoon proportions, both as a result of collecting from

nurseries and by the generosity of people coming from America, Holland, and Brazil. The latest group, brought by friends from Brazil, numbered more than 200 plants, all carried on the flight in a hat box and arriving in perfect condition. The glass house is now bulging with orchids and a new glass house is planned to make room for the continuing work with seeds.

The library mentioned above has been another project of particular importance in the last year. The collection of books grew rapidly as a result of many generous donations in India and abroad, and a separate library room with protective cabinets became necessary for the preservation of the books so that they could be accessible to everyone. This has been completed just enough to be in use, though finishing has stopped for lack of funds.

In speaking at various times about Her vision of the future gardens surrounding the Matrimandir, the Mother spoke very clearly about the presence of waterways in the landscape. This year, through the combined interest of workers here and friends in America, the many-faceted work of water gardening has begun with the collection of various aquatic plants and many beautiful water lilies. Hand in hand with this has been the beginning of water ecology studies, the collection and observation of various kinds of koi and other water animals, and the experimental construction of a natural pond according to an ancient Chinese method. This method utilizes ordinary clay with a layer of organic matter sandwiched between. As the organic matter decomposes, the bacteria fill microscopic fissures in the clay and a completely watertight seal is effected. This creates a totally natural setting which induces a spontaneous ecological balance. In the future we hope to experiment with modern sealing materials available in America, which achieve the same results but require much less labour.

All of these activities taking place in the Nursery, though seemingly diverse, have a single purpose, which is to provide a firm basis in experience, knowledge and materials for the Matrimandir Gardens. The area of the Gardens will eventually encompass approximately 125 acres in a wide circular belt surrounding the inner angle of the city formed by the Matrimandir, the Banyan tree, and the Lotus Urn.

Forming the structure of the sphere of the Matrimandir are 4 pillars approximately facing the cardinal points. To each of these pillars the Mother gave the name of one of the four aspects of the Supreme Mother: North is Mahakali, East is Mahalakshmi, South is Maheshwari, and West is Mahasaraswati. To each of these aspects she gave corresponding colours: Mahakali is red and gold, Mahalakshmi pink, lavender and pale green, Maheshwari is gold and blue, and Mahasaraswati is red and white. According to the present outline, which is based on a sketch made by the Mother, the area closest to centre will be fairly open, containing only the waterways and 12 Gardens, which the Mother named Existence, Consciousness, Bliss, Light, Life, Power, Riches, Utility, Progress, Youth, Harmony and Perfection, with the Garden of Unity surrounding the Banyan tree. Outside of this inner area will be a ring of trees, shrubs and groundcover plants beginning with low trees widely spaced and becoming more dense and tall toward the outer circumference. The first trees to form this wooded belt were put into the ground on November 24, 1973, in the area extending from the pillar of Mahasaraswati. Since the winter of 1973-74, when the first large plantation was completed in the Mahakali quadrant, more than 700 trees have been planted in a continuing band into the area of Mahasaraswati and another large section in Maheshwari, where the normally flat land has been gently contoured to form low rolling hills. During the winter of 1975-76 several sections, including both sides of the present access road to the Matrimandir, have been planted linking the Mahasaraswati and Maheshwari areas. Development of the east side of Mahalakshmi awaits further land purchases.

Position and choice of the trees going into the outer gardens has followed only one exterior plan, and that is the colour guide that was given to each pillar by the Mother. The rest is done with a minimum of formal planning; preliminary studies are made of the possibilities for each area in an effort to become as familiar as possible with the characteristics and requirements of the plants, but the actual placement is spontaneous. For each one of these trees the same preparation and care must be given as in the Nursery. Pits must be dug and the red clay replaced by topsoil and compost. As the area is completely exposed to animals and weather, a protective basket must be woven and placed around the plant until it is tall enough to survive alone. The water system consists of two relatively shallow wells and two storage tanks. From these tanks water is dispersed through underground pipes over much of the Garden, but in outlying areas it must be carried by wheelbarrow and bullock cart. The work is challenging and the conditions and lack of equipment always a handicap, but the results more than compensate for this. In this year's unusually heavy monsoon rains we saw how even the initial contouring retained great quantities of water that usually run off, carrying away inches of topsoil every year. After only 3 years many of the trees in the Mahakali area are more than 10 feet high and in many areas are already dotting the hills with spots of colour. Each year new and greater numbers of birds are attracted to the protection of the trees. It is especially encouraging to see that so many of the new introduced species, many of which have been sent to us as a result of the seed-exchange programme, have established themselves easily, obviously happy with their new home. But more fulfilling than all is to climb to the top of Matrimandir and to view from that height the future forest, now only small dots of green but already giving new life to the arid plain.

It is impossible to describe in words more than a surface image of any aspect of Auroville, for it is something living and unique which must be experienced by each one according to the truth of his own inner being. This is especially true of the Matrimandir and the life and work which surround it.

We invite all of goodwill to share with us in any way in the manifestation of the soul of Auroville, the Matrimandir and the Gardens.

(date unknown)

Incident at the Nursery

One evening when we were walking through the Matrimandir Nursery and talking of the work to be done the next day, suddenly Sundarmurti (the head gardener) threw me down on the ground. This was extraordinary behaviour, for in those early days it was not even customary for the Tamil boys to shake hands or embrace these strange white people. Lifting me up from the ground he apologized and said, "Narad, you were about to step on the head of a Krait". This snake, which is more venomous than vipers or cobras, could well have killed me. Sundarmurti saved my life.

Sundarmurti

In contrast....

One day, as Toine was walking up from Kottakarai and coming up to the back entrance of the Nursery, he saw Sundarmurti and some of the boys gorging themselves on mangoes they had stolen from the Nursery. There was a huge basket full, so I wrote to Mother.

She replied, "If it is only mangoes they can be forgiven this time".

Narad

mid 1990s

A request for helpers at the MM Gardens:

To all Aurovilians, Ashramites, Golden Chain Members and Devotees, as the Matrimandir nears completion the work on the Gardens (which Mother said was as important as the structure) is accelerating. In the next few months we will plant thousands of square metres of grass around the Matrimandir, which will also require careful and regular maintenance afterwards.

We invite all those who sincerely aspire to see the Gardens manifest to take part in the grass planting, composting and weeding projects underway. There is a tremendous amount of work to be done during and immediately following this monsoon season, and it is an opportunity for all of us to come together in a spirit of harmonious collaboration and karma yoga. All help will be gratefully received. If you would like to come in the mornings, we work from 8:00 a.m. to 12:00 p.m. with a five minute concentration under the Banyan tree from 8:05 to 8:10 to ask Mother's blessings and protection for the day's work. Other timings are also available.

A group of Golden Chain volunteers from the Sri Aurobindo Ashram

The work consists of removing weeds and nut grass, helping in the compost area, leveling and cleaning sections of the Park, and filling in excavated areas with a soil/compost mix prior to planting seeds, sod, and rhizomes. Much of the work is not physically demanding, but it is usually in full sun so hats and skin protection are advisable.

A further request is for someone who would be interested in learning and eventually supervising the many aspects of turf management, such as maintenance of equipment, scheduling cutting times and heights, fertilizing, weed control and data collection on species and hybrids under trial at the Gardens.

If you would like to help please contact Narad at 989·424-8711 or at Ashirwad on Chetty St., just a few hundred feet from the Ashram gate, across the canal, or telephone Michael Tait at the Matrimandir Office at 2623548.

At the Service of Truth,
Narad (for the Matrimandir Gardens)

18 February 1999

Narad writes to Amrita Iriyama who had been attacked and narrowly escaped being thrown down a deep well-hole by his assailants:

Dear Amrit,

We have just heard through an email from Julian Lines of your terrible ordeal.

Mary Helen and I both send you our prayers for a quick recovery and for Mother's protection. You are never far from us in our thoughts or in our prayers and in our remembrance of you as a pillar of Their work in Auroville.

With our love,
In Their Light,

Narad

2 February 2001

Note to all concerned with the Matrimandir:
Dear Matrimandir Workers, Devotees and Disciples of Mother and Sri Aurobindo,

I write today to offer my gratitude for the Matrimandir Journals we have been receiving. They are truly an inspiration to read and are done with a deep inner sensitivity, aspiration for Truth, and artistic sensitivity.

Though in bodily form far from you, a large part of my soul is there at the Matrimandir. As we study Savitri each day and work towards completion of the Savitri "Lexicon", still a year away, my thoughts and prayers are with you and with our many brothers and sisters in the ashram for the collective reception of the Supramental force.

Mary Helen reads Savitri every evening, and the other night a few lines leaped out at me because I felt the Matrimandir in them and thought perhaps that Sri Aurobindo had written them foreseeing its realisation.

From The Book of the Divine Mother:

> In the passion of its solitary dream
> It lay like a closed soundless oratory
> Where sleeps a consecrated argent floor
> Lit by a single and untrembling ray
> And an invisible Presence kneels in prayer.

Lastly, I recently read that one of the Gardens was to begin and I recalled a conversation with Mother which I would like to share with you. At one point She said to me: "I would like you to begin with the Garden of Unity". After Mother told me this I started regular pruning of the dead branches of the Banyan tree, and brought down the aerial roots to brace the large branches that were extending outwards without support. I hope the Gardens can begin with Unity.

> Thank you again for remembering us.
> In Their Light and Love
>
> Narad

undated letter

Dear Friends,

You ask how I feel about trees. In February of this year I spent hours with Leonard and Nadia going through "Flowers and Their Messages" to select trees that would be most suitable for the Matrimandir Gardens. Trees are the Guardian Presences, the calm Protectors who offer their cooling shade and strength to all who walk under their welcoming branches. To know how I feel about trees one has only to stand under the 'Service Tree' at the Samadhi or the Banyan of the Matrimandir.

Having said this, I would like also to add that the two most important things for me are harmony and goodwill among all who aspire to realise the Gardens. Only with these can the beginning of a true unity be achieved. With the Divine Grace that many of us feel is giving us yet another opportunity to manifest the Gardens of the Matrimandir comes also the necessity of oneness built on love for Mother and the souls who have been called to Her work.

Let us trust in the Divine, rise above personalities, offering constructive ideas, but not pointing a finger at specific

individuals. Can we also accept Mother's words that the Lord is building Her creation and resolve to work together in a spirit of collaboration. The Gardens will be built according to the Divine Will.

At the Service of Truth,
Narad

30 July 2002

Correspondence with John Harper, Michael Bonke and Alain Grandcolas:

Dear John,

I am grateful for your letter and the love and aspiration you express. I don't know how I can help realise the Gardens at this time. The reports I get from people is that there is such a lack of harmony and so great a discord that at this point in my life I would not be able to work in such an atmosphere.

I am enclosing a few recent letters in reply to letters from Michael Bonke and Alain Grandcolas. I would also like to tell all those who sincerely wish to realise Mother's vision of the Matrimandir Gardens that they only have to follow what is in Huta's book. Mother has spoken to her, to me, to Mary Helen, drawn sketches, and more than once has emphatically and specifically stated that the Matrimandir would be on an island, there would be the lake and the park, etc, etc. This should be enough for those who are sincere.

My love to you, Amrit and all who aspire to manifest Her vision.

At Their Feet,
Narad

Subject: Matrimandir Gardens
Michael,

It is now past midnight but sleep does not come since it seems I am guided to tell you more about the Gardens. When Mary Helen asked Mother specifically about the twelve Gardens and Mother replied that it will be in the Japanese way, we understood immediately that there would be no artificiality. We have been to Japan more than once and when Mary Helen was young she lived there with her family for more than a year. We have been fortunate in that when we visited, the Japanese people took us into their hearts and allowed us to go "behind the scenes" where Westerners were never allowed. In the Bonsai Village outside Tokyo, Chali, then a little girl, was idolized by the Japanese ladies and we were shown a rare view of the meticulous care of bonsai, handed down from generation to generation, seeing plants that were never or rarely ever seen by the public. In Kyoto I also had a wonderful experience which I will tell you about one day. It is a somewhat lengthy story so I cannot write of it now, but it certainly gave me an understanding of time and maturation with plants and gardens.

There is hardly any artificiality in Japanese gardens, with the exception of some of the pruning practices which Mother did not favour. So we can see that the Gardens of the Matrimandir must develop organically and, what is essential in karma yoga, is that Aurovilians offer their physical bodies for the work. I often felt that the first group of "pioneer" Aurovilians were Mother's wedges to "open up the earth" for the manifestation that was to come. Perhaps we were not much more than that!

I have a feeling that my letter to Alain Grandcolas might not have made it into your hands, so I share it with you below. In Mother's Love,
Narad

Dear Alain,

The text of the article you sent, notwithstanding the ever-changing design of the twelve Gardens, is the one that guided me through the work of the outer Gardens when it was not possible to begin the twelve Gardens due to construction. The area for the 'Outer Gardens' was measured off and I planted two quadrants and began the third, according to the four aspects of the Mother, using flowering trees or foliage that represented the colours of Mahalakshmi, Mahasaraswati, Maheshwari and Mahakali. I believe the text you sent came directly from Roger's group or Roger himself. Many of these Garden areas were planted in trees from the two areas of the world that in our tests acclimatized most readily, northern Australia, specifically Queensland and Townsville, and from Brazil and areas of South America.

You asked in a previous letter if I might share any personal memories of things Mother said about the Gardens. One I specifically remember that She said to me was: "I would like you to begin with the Garden of Unity". It was at this time that I worked with Sundarmurti to guide the aerial roots of the Banyan tree to root into the earth to support the limbs that had extended so far that they were in danger of breaking under their own weight.

Although I am inundated by work I have not forgotten Serge's request and am slowly gathering together whatever reports, correspondences, etc, I have on the development of the Matrimandir Gardens.

In Mother's Love and Light,

Narad

P.S. After Mother sent word that She wanted me to come and build the Gardens of the Matrimandir I met Roger, and although I felt that the Gardens as a whole would be something vast (and with the Outer Gardens they certainly are), I never had a cross word with Roger. There was always a feeling of harmony. A number of times he came to me and told me that he had designed a Garden much larger or expanded the size of another Garden. As I never had the vision of what the Gardens would look like, only the ever-burning words of Mother that "one must know how to move from consciousness to consciousness", I felt that the design would come through harmony and be built through consciousness. Still, as a lady, Manuele has written to me, there must be a basis of horticultural knowledge to realise the work, and that is why Mother mentioned to Satprem in the Agenda that I had studied landscaping in the USA. I began at the age of 11, cutting lawns and maintaining people's gardens. At any rate, if those "in charge" would begin clearing out the hundreds of teak trees that do not belong in the Outer Gardens and do a general clean-up, it would go a long way towards clarifying what remains and needs attention. Please excuse me if I am too frank.

Part of a letter: You certainly express the disharmony at Matrimandir in very strong words and I do not for a moment doubt anything you say. I have seen and lived in very dark periods in Auroville and I truly believe that Mother lifted me out of the situation at a critical time. One day I will tell you much more about my meetings with Nolini and his words about Auroville. For now, I await Her adesh, and am certain I will receive it according to my openness. I am still going through a very difficult time with Mary Helen's passing, but the Grace is ever present and holds me up.

To: Michael Bonke

The city of Auroville, township if you will, is a field of vast experiment, fueled with the energy, aspiration and movement of thousands and, like the human mind, one may use the well-known analogy of a radio tuned in to all stations at once.

When we wish to communicate with our soul, the Divine Presence seated in the heart, by entering the Matrimandir Gardens and the inner room, the sanctuary, we need a filter to prepare us and calm the busy hum of mental and physical activity natural to a city that is an experiment in human unity and so many other fields of higher endeavour. The outer Gardens or "park" that Mother has sketched, written about and spoken of so many times, is that filter.

In its atmosphere of beauty, harmony and tranquility one sheds the accumulations of the city's energy for a moment, preparing to experience "physically and concretely" the significance of one or more of the Matrimandir Gardens en route to the "closed soundless oratory" where we await the higher Guidance that speaks directly to the Divine within.

From the moment we enter this area nothing is artificial, all is natural, lakes, trees, plants, rocks, grasses, all in the Japanese way, but not totally Japanese, because Mother did not approve of the distortion of plants by certain pruning techniques.

This is my inner feeling - harmony, intense beauty, peacefulness, a pervading sweetness that encompasses preparing us to go within and lifts us out of our narrow human ways into the infinity of the Divine's Love.

Narad

23 October 2002

Alain Grandcolas refers to a reply from Gilles Guigan:

Dear Narad,
Please find in the attached file Gilles' plans for the Matrimandir Gardens.
Bien amicalement, Alain

24 October 2002

Narad writes back to Alain G:

Dear Alain,

Please thank Gilles for his excellent detailed reply. I now understand exactly what his plan is and his drawing has also helped as well. I think it is an excellent plan but it does raise some further questions that are perhaps more pertinent to design and the "great beauty" Mother spoke about to me.
1. Firstly, no trees in the Gardens? If only pots with a few plants this then may be a nice architectural presentation but it is not a garden.
2. Or are the "Gardens" still very small and trees are all around the outer Gardens area? As you can understand, there must be shade in such a tropical climate.
3. Is the entire area for the "inner gardens" to be excavated

to the necessary depth in order to bring in the sand? Is this not also a cost factor that can be considerable?
4. I will look into the geotextile question for I feel that Gilles' idea needs to be pursued.
5. Could someone also do a cost estimate if the area was even deeper since excavating equipment is already in place? Is there someone who can do a cost/benefit analysis? I'm sure Gilles has probably considered this already.
6. Please tell Gilles that in one letter I have learned a lot. As I said, I am not an engineer, but the concept of preservation of water is most important and I will help in any way I can with research on the geotextile.

In Mother's Love,

Narad

13 February 2003

Letter from Narad to Roger:

> Garden of Unity
>
> Dear Roger,
>
> I am deeply disappointed by your refusal to meet with me and Paolo in a spirit of oneness to begin the Garden of Unity on February 15th. In my previous letter I had written the following:
>
> I had a very good talk with Paolo. Unfortunately he leaves on the 16th but he is willing to come out on the 15th and the three of us could break ground for the Garden of Unity, which Mother wanted me to begin first. Paolo has no preconceived ideas and I also have none, so I think this could be a great leap forward and an opportunity to dissipate the hostility and distrust in Auroville as it will show our wideness and willingness to work together.
>
> Subsequently I had also told Jacqueline on the telephone that Paolo had agreed to come in a spirit of harmony and collaboration and without a personal agenda for the design of the Garden. Your statement to me therefore that Paolo must change his attitude before you can work with him seems to me to be without substance or validity. Mother gave you the sacred work as the architect of Auroville and I believe She has given us yet another opportunity to begin the work of the Gardens in peace. I also believe that you have the capacity to embrace and encompass many different concepts and show the way to unity without compromising the integrity of your vision.
>
> Mother wants us to work together now, and especially for

you and Paolo to collaborate. I have spent these last months devoting myself to that end, praying constantly to Mother for guidance. I hope you will reconsider your refusal and agree to meet on the 15th as Paolo leaves on the 16th. I would be grateful to know that a true beginning would be made and the efforts and prayers of so many Aurovilians have not been in vain.

I will be in Trichy the entire day of the 14th for a visit to a garden where many plants are being kept for me, the gift of friends throughout the world for the future gardens of Auroville and the Ashram. However, I would cancel this trip if your schedule precluded your meeting on the 15th and you had to meet on the 14th. Please let me know as soon as possible.

I am prepared to work together for the manifestation of the Matrimandir Gardens but it is essential that we do the following:

1. Find a point on which we can all agree. Can we say this is the importance of beginning the Matrimandir Gardens now?
2. Each of us must rise just a little above our present position in an aspiration to truly unite our efforts and find the harmony that is urgently needed.
3. Begin the work with the full trust that the Mother will guide us, and surrender to the Divine Will, having faith that all our difficulties will be resolved by the Grace.

Please know that you have my respect and willingness to collaborate and realise the beauty and splendour that is waiting to descend.

In the Mother's Love,
Narad

(13 February 2003) **Note from Roger's partner, Jacqueline, to Narad**:

Subject: Re: Garden of Unity
Dear Narad,

I just read your email, and I feel sad.... First, Roger has left half an hour ago to join a meeting with some members of the Governing Board and the residents of Auroville. He will have a dinner at the Solar Kitchen and another meeting with Harald Kraft, who is going to present his studies on the lake. He will be back late I suppose and will not be able to read your email before tomorrow morning... Tomorow he has to be at 9 am at Matrimandir for the visit of the Board and then he will have meetings the full day with the different working groups in Auroville, and it will be the same for the next day...as he told you on the phone. But the main reason of my sadness is resumed in your first sentence. I was just expecting and praying that you will not so quickly put Roger in the position of the 'bad guy' who refuses to make the opening towards unity. It is difficult to write all I would like to tell you...But please, Narad, the 'things' are not so simple... Let us try to meet one more time and speak.

With a lot of love and regards,

Jacqueline

Letter to Roger and Jacqueline from Narad:

Dear Roger and Jacqueline,

Thank you for your letter and the 'Guidelines' from Alain. As you may know I have chosen not to correspond with Alain for a while as I have found his arrogant and condescending attitude far from the harmony we seek to achieve. Others are writing to me, however, so I have been kept informed of developments.

I am in agreement with you, Roger, in that the parameters of the 'Guidelines' are too restrictive and narrow, although it is basically a good effort from Alain. There are certain terms as well as sentence structures that would not be generally used in English, but other than that the concept appears too rigid, and I personally do not agree with the idea of 'outside' landscape architects to come in (regardless of their expertise) unless there are some who have an inner opening to the Divine consciousness and, if not the path and vision of the Mother and Sri Aurobindo, at least an affinity toward the ideals of Auroville.

I don't know where Alain has had the vision to express some things, such as "**Elements sculptural** should be rather more evocative than descriptive".

"Most of the elements in the Garden must be **flexible and mobile**". Does this indicate that there are to be no permanent plantings or plantings in the soil, only containers in each Garden? I would appreciate clarification of this.

"**Few flowers**. Their presence may be exquisite and the areas reserved for them may not be big". Does this sentence imply 'cannot' rather than 'may not'? If it is 'may not' then it is open to other possibilities, if 'cannot', then it is clearly understood that there can be no change.

Is there to be nothing of the Japanese way?

I personally felt that the work of Mark and Nadia and the group that was formed had the aspiration to open to that which Mother wants to manifest.

There could be much more to add but let me leave it at that for the moment.

I have good news about the grass and am copying my letter to Michael and Andy for your records. Sadly, there has been no response from anyone for one month!

I shall see you much sooner than originally anticipated.

In Mother's Love,

Narad

25 May 2003

Letter from Narad to Amrita:

Subject: Daniel address

Dear Amrit,

It is early Sunday morning and the wild mallards have been sitting by my door waiting for me to feed them. The sun is breaking through clouds after weeks of heavy rain. The late azaleas are in bloom and in a few days hydrangeas will reach their peak with an intense and breathtaking display of purple, pink, blue and white in large, dense heads or delicate "lace caps" with their marvel of symmetry and design.

I am very grateful that you have taken up the work of the plumerias outside the Nursery. I have received via email some of the photos from Elke. It is an inner reward to see that so many beautiful crosses have matured and survive. Heinz would like me to name the finest of these and I will do so in time. However, they will need to be registered with the Plumeria Society of America, and one has to fill out a form supplying a photo and complete description of each cultivar. I think you could be of great help here for the future of the Matrimandir Gardens, for I think we could make many thousands of dollars selling named cultivars from the Matrimandir and also spread the beauty of the plants and the force contained within all over the world. If you could begin propagating and protecting *P.caracasana*, it would bring in thousands of dollars alone as collectors from many countries are seeking it. With all the layerings that have been stolen from the gardens (Heinz has confronted people in Bangalore and elsewhere, looking them in the eye and telling them they stole the cuttings from the Matrimandir) our window of opportunity is not great, but it is there. The tree is in very poor health, and Heinz tells me that he has come at times and made twenty layerings, only to return and find one or two left. If you are interested in getting a number of plants started so that layerings could be made (I understand that it is very difficult to do root cuttings) I believe we could get around $50 per rooted cutting and hundreds could be sold. Perhaps I could notify the various plumeria societies in the future when ample stock is ready, and their members could send orders directly to you or you could send cuttings in lots to a distributor here. There would be less profit but it would be much easier. I hope you will consider the idea.

I am also gratified that you have come to appreciate Heinz. He has a brilliant mind, and has a solid grasp of many aspects of horticulture and extensive knowledge in many other areas. Our trip to his Ashram was really a special occasion, with Andreas (another Swiss), Kabul, Heinz and myself. Yes, his unbridled vital nature can be draining, but he is a rare soul and I have long felt that Mother sent him to me as one of those who in the future might be an integral part of the Gardens. When Mary Helen left I received the most beautiful letter from him. We had never met or corresponded previously and this extraordinary pouring out of his soul marked him as one of Hers regardless of where he is and who his guru might be, for his guru, too, worships The Mother and has written me a truly beautiful letter as well. As for the vital exuberance, it can be draining, but towards the end of my last visit we had many moments of quiet together. I simply would ask him to sit with me for a few minutes and concentrate or meditate, and I think this would be a good thing for you to do together as well. He will immediately respond, and for a while the vibrational aura will change until he ramps up once again. But you see, I know a little about the vital (as they would say in India), isn't it? As to Kabul, he is one with us and no more needs to be said. You can be certain that others will come in time when Aurovilians are ready, but it is a blessing to see these first heralds in physical form. Please keep them both close.

I can add nothing to your second paragraph. Everything you write is accurate. Yes, continue quietly the work you speak of in paragraph three. Please tell Zulfi that I feel Mother's blessings are with him for this work, and I will pray to Her that Her grace might shower upon him.

I have much more to write you but it will have to wait for another letter as it concerns things about the Matrimandir, and I don't want to add it to this lengthy letter. Here are the email addresses. I am sure they will both reply promptly and will look forward to your visit. Daniel and Heinz have already met at Nong Nooch. Daniel and Chika live in Chiang Mai, August in Bangkok. Both are teachers.

One last story to share and I'll sign off. Daniel goes to a meditation retreat with a Zen master once a year. They meditate for ten hours and then all file before the Master after the meditation. When Daniel came to him he said: "Ah, you are from a different nest, but welcome!"

Daniel and Chika Wilms
Prem Center, Chiang Mai, Thailand
Love,
Narad

undated

Amrita

Here follows an article written by Amrit, earlier known as Howard Iriyama, and one of the most dedicated workers in the Matrimandir Gardens and Nursery. He was one of the first to settle in the Matrimandir Gardens Nursery, and just as all of us had to suffer the trials of thieves, heat, poor food, etc, Amrit was extremely competent with a brilliant mind, and his work with us remains for me a highlight of harmony with Mother's true child. So much could be said about his quiet nature, his willingness to do any work, his endurance and more, but let his words now speak.In Gratitude,
Narad

27 May 2003

Reply to Narad from Amrita:
Subject: Daniel address

Dear Narad,

First of all, I'm truly sorry to hear about both your brother and Daniel. For some reason, there have been quite a few people I know who have been having similar problems. I don't know really what is happening. I hope at least they will become better. I know physically, psychologically and spiritually what a test this must be for all. Some only become depressed and bitter, but for others, I think more spiritually mature, it becomes an opportunity to rise above pain, fear and hopelessness into a greater light and joy. I think Mary Helen was such a person. My prayers and best wishes for both your brother and Daniel. It makes one realise more and more how precious good health and life are, and that we must be grateful and joyful for all that we have been given. Very frankly Narad, for many years now, a kind of inner happiness and joy have slowly been unfolding and growing in the heart. Even though sometimes shadows pass over that happiness, yet always it seems to be there, and I have realised how such a simple thing can be so wonderful. Because deep inside, it is rooted in a kind of love and ananda.

About the possibilities of selling the plumerias and the *P.caracasana*, it definitely has potentials. However, for several reasons, 1. the political situation in Auroville and

2. the CAG Government audit of accounts in Auroville and Matrimandir, it has become more difficult to engage in commercial transactions. One has to be very careful. We used to have a commercial outlet called "Blossoming", but that was closed down some years back. So we don't have anymore any official channel through which to conduct this type of business. On the other hand, we should find some way to help support the Nursery and Gardens when they come. But given the very touchy situation both with the Government and the Community, and its relationship with the Government, one has to be very careful about anything that could be misinterpreted. I think you understand what I am saying. This does not mean that in the future something is not possible. Until the situation at Matrimandir clarifies, almost everything has been put on hold. The exchanges with Heinz and Michael at Nong Nooch have been no problem, because there have been no financial transactions involved, only plant exchanges. I think one can slowly work towards this possibility in the future.

I`m glad you received the plumeria photos from Elke. She did a good job. Some of the flowers are remarkably beautiful, aren't they? I'll try to plant more *P.caracasana* in the Nursery.

I also felt that with yourself, Heinz, N.N. Michael, Kabul, etc, whether directly or indirectly, a kind of group network is forming for the Matrimandir Gardens. Maybe this is also why I felt moved to leave the other responsibilities and concentrate only on the Nursery. But very frankly, when I witness the dissension at Matrimandir, I think Auroville is not ready yet for the beauty that Mother wishes to manifest here, though much has even then manifested, perhaps in spite of the people. So I know there's always hope. I hope before leaving this body, I will see something.

As for Heinz, this last time I didn't find him so draining, maybe because I myself took more interest in what he was doing, and also have come to appreciate him more. It takes me time to warm up to people, especially talkative people. I had visited his Ashram many years back with a friend, though I didn't know Heinz at the time. His Guru had also come to the Nursery, as we were quite generous with the plumerias and gave his Ashram many plants.

When we go to Thailand, I'd definitely like to meet August and Daniel and Chika. I'd always wondered why they chose Thailand as their home, though after being there for only 3 days, I think I understand. I sympathize with Daniel's interest in Zen, as I was myself in a Zen monastery in Japan for some time. I have a great respect for that path.

I could say more about the situation at Matrimandir, but I find it so distressing that I have avoided saying much. The Nursery has by and large been relatively peaceful, not fully untouched by the turmoil, but still better than most places. We're just about to start improving and renovating the small lab used primarily for Phalaenopsis propagation from seed. At the same time, we're trying to shift more and more orchids to the Matrimandir site, out of the Nursery. I think with Heinz', yours and others' help, we will gradually and slowly again begin to build up our collection of plants, as well as continue our work with the identification and cataloguing of different species and varieties.

Anyway, take care, love,

Amrit

31 May 2003

Narad replies to Amrita:

Subject: Matrimandir Action Committee

Amrit,
Are you getting these email treatises? They are incredibly dark. I can forward the latest if you don't have it.

Here also, a note from Julian I think you should see.

Dear Narad,

Seeing everything green and flowering reminds me of you!

How was your return from India? I would really love to hear about your reflections on your trip.

I met Kireet Joshi in Washington DC last month and he is deeply troubled in a number of areas concerning Auroville, but Matrimandir weighs most heavily.

Things are difficult 'within' just now so please bear with me and eventually I'll write more.

With my love at Their Feet,

Narad

29 July 2003

Remembering Daniel Wilms - Disciple, Friend and Brother

Daniel Wilms with Sundarmurti

To All Disciples of the Mother and Sri Aurobindo:

Today, on my birthday, I received a letter from Daniel Wilms' wife, Chika, informing me of his passing last night, the day on which I had sent him some poems, as he had been so strongly in my consciousness this past week.

Daniel first came to the Matrimandir Gardens through my friend and elder brother, Louis Allen, with whom he had been working at the Lake Estate. When Daniel began work at the Matrimandir Gardens Nursery he did everything with love and such a great joy that one was uplifted to be in his atmosphere. He was an indefatigable worker who never refused a task and took little rest, even in the heat of summer. I have many photographs of those days with seekers who came from the U.S., Holland, France, Germany and other parts of the world, all aspiring to realise Mother's words to me about the Matrimandir Gardens: "It must be a thing of great beauty, of such a beauty that when men enter they will say, 'Ah, this is it', and will experience physically and concretely, the significance of each Garden", words which all of you have probably often read.

It was to be more than twenty years before I would see Daniel again. He had suffered much in his life and wandered for many years before he found Chika and was blessed with a daughter, Johanna, but the inner joy and love for Mother and Sri Aurobindo never left him. I had been invited to be a guest of the Nong Nooch Tropical Garden in Thailand, south of Bangkok. Daniel made a twenty hour train trip from his home in Chang Mai in the north to join me at the garden, where he was also welcomed. The moment we met all the years fell away and it was as if we two children of the Mother had never been apart. We spent three wonderful days among the flowers we loved, swam in blue waters under a waxing moon, and shared a oneness that must have been the recognition of soul-meetings in past lives.

After our stay in Nong Nooch we traveled to Bangkok to meet August Timmermans (Guus), another early and deeply dedicated member of the Matrimandir Gardens staff and a regular at the music evenings in our home. I had corresponded briefly with August concerning Savitri, and our meeting in Bangkok, again after more than twenty years, brought back to the three of us the joys and difficulties of those pioneering days, but most of all the shared experience of the tremendous force and love Mother was bringing down for the manifestation of Her vision of Auroville and the Matrimandir.

Shortly after our meeting in Thailand Daniel was diagnosed with a cancerous brain tumor. This was about the same time that my youngest brother was also diagnosed for a similar condition. Surgery was performed, but Daniel's tumor grew back rapidly and he had to undergo radiation therapy. I kept in touch with him during these months and was able to send him the sand from the Samadhi, Blessing Packets and words from the Mother, one of which I quote here:

> "...remember that I am present in thee
> and lose not hope;
> each effort, each grief,
> each joy and each pang,
> each call of thy heart,
> each aspiration of thy soul, ...
> all, all without exception, ...
> LEAD THEE TOWARDS ME..."
>
> The Mother

I conclude this tribute to a disciple with the following remembrances that will remain with me for all time.

In our small room at the Botanical Gardens I had placed Blessing Packets by a lamp to remember Mother and Sri Aurobindo in waking and before sleep. On coming into the room I found Daniel prostrate before Them in deep meditation.

When we were in Thailand Daniel shared with me the following experience. He would go once a year to a meditation retreat with a Zen master where he would meditate with others for ten hours a day and afterwards all would pass before the Master. When Daniel approached, the Master spoke to him and said: "Ah, you are from a different nest, but welcome!"

On this day a brother in the Ashram has offered flowers for me on the Samadhi. I, in turn, offer them for Daniel at the Feet of the Mother and Sri Aurobindo.

Narad

31 January 2005

Interview with Narad on the Matrimandir Gardens by Auroville Today

There is no conflict. Our work differs in its focus but that is the only difference. We have the greatest respect for each other and I always visit some Green Belt communities every time I return. The Matrimandir Gardens are something quite different in aim and expression from the afforestation work, though all work with and for the earth is essentially one. The Gardens will be intense in the concentration and power of beauty they must manifest but in size a small fraction of the Green Belt around the township. The planting of indigenous species and the return of the natural forest has been the aspiration and aim of those who have worked in the Green Belt since its inception. I am in full accord with this plan, but there are also some excellent tree species that were introduced from other areas of the world that accept the same climatic conditions and add to the beauty and diversity of the forest, and these are being cared for as well. When the climate changes with the Supramental force fully active on earth we will see wonderful changes in the plant world. That is, however, something of the future of which we cannot now speak.

Some may not be aware that in the early years from 1970 on we grew thousands of trees at the Matrimandir Gardens Nursery for planting throughout the Green Belt. Many of the species we planted were indigenous to South India, collected on visits to forest and jungles with some of the finest Conservators of Forests in the Indian Government. One day I could send you copies of some of their correspondence after visiting the Matrimandir Gardens in its infancy.

We also grew thousands of "Work" (*Acacia auriculiformis*) trees to act as 'nurse' trees, opening up the soil, building up the forest litter and providing shade cover for the slower growing indigenous species. This has become a beautiful example of successive regeneration. As the indigenous trees create a dense canopy the 'Work' trees slowly die out but their seeds germinate in barren areas carrying on the 'work!'.

Last year I had the opportunity to walk through some of the forests of the Green Belt. I was amazed to see the amount of work accomplished by these rugged pioneers who are realising and have already realised to a vast extent the Green

Belt, which is creating the beneficial microclimate Mother envisaged. I feel, unfortunately, that their sincere efforts have been largely ignored by the greater body of Auroville. Just as I made lifelong contacts with Conservators of Forests, the French Institute, and other horticultural institutions, so too have they continued this invaluable collaboration with scientists and other plant specialists, exchanging seeds, knowledge and experiences for the benefit of Auroville and Mother India.

A walk through the Green Belt with Jean of 'Two Banyans' and Patrick of 'Revelation' was truly a revelation for me. Jean pointed out tree after tree received from the Matrimandir Gardens Nursery, now towering giants in a mixed forest, and along with indigenous species, thriving only on the yearly rainfall. I walked through Patrick's cow barn and compost area and never saw one fly! Through his association with one of the Vector Control experts they introduced an ant that lives on the fly eggs and keeps the place clean. I also acknowledge humbly that their knowledge of all the forest species, trees, shrubs, vines, far exceeds all that I learned in the first twelve years of Auroville. To know that two species of civet cat have returned to the forest, eat the berries of native shrubs and vines, distribute the seeds to germinate in other places, to realise that when we arrived in Auroville there were approximately 30 species of birds and today's count is in excess of 120, is a tribute to all the communities of Auroville who have devoted themselves to planting trees and flowering plants. Not only that, but the work of building check dams and allowing the water to percolate into the aquifers instead of running out to sea continues, and today there are large areas where the rainwater is fully contained. Lastly, I bow to the knowledge the workers of the Green Belt have developed in the field of ecology and water conservation.

With the tragic death of Sydo I pray that the community of Auroville will visit the Green Belt areas, learn of the first South Indian Eagle to nest there in more than 100 years, who flies two metres above the road in the early evening, speak with the Green Belt foresters who are versed in so many subjects. There are many others in the Green Belt who have spoken to me or with whom I have visited or met briefly, and all have my profoundest respect. I pray too that Auroville will help to further this work with funding to continue the work and protect the forests as well as the Aurovilians who work there. Mother's charge to me to create a beauty never seen on earth before has yet to be realised, but the Green Belt is already on the way towards accomplishing Her vision.

The morning after Sydo's death we transplanted about 18 new varieties of lotus from seed that was sent to me by Peter Slocum, the owner of the largest water lily and lotus firm in America. Mary Helen and I had met him on our world tour of plant collecting in 1977. I wrote him saying that I wanted to bring seeds of the finest lotus hybrids created during the last twenty-five years for Auroville and the Ashram. I wrote him on my letterhead, Tropical Plant Specialists, and signed my name Richard M. Eggenberger. Peter replied within a few days and said: "Of course I remember you, Narad". He then sent me the seeds of their most beautiful cultivars.

We planted these in one of the Ashram gardens and Kabul of the Ashram has worked out the best method for propagation. In just over two months from seed the lotuses have developed excellent tubers and we were able to take 22 plants to Kireet at Gaia's Garden. As these tubers increase and divide and are shared in gardens throughout Auroville, I would like it to be known that they were planted to honour Sydo, that all might remember him in the beauty and fragrance of the flowers.

March 2005

Extract from an interview with Narad by AV Today

"I have faith that everything will be done according to the Divine's Will," says Narad, who was asked by Mother in 1969 to design and build the Matrimandir Gardens. In the early 1970s he set up the Matrimandir Nursery for collecting, studying and propagating many rare and beautiful plants from all over the world. Twelve years later he returned to the U.S. where he continued to extend his deep knowledge of plants and trees and to collect specimens for the Ashram and Auroville.

He has revisited regularly. On his most recent visit he spoke about his concerns for the Banyan Tree by Matrimandir and about his continuing involvement in finding new varieties of plants for the Gardens.

AV Today: Do you feel you have a special relationship with the Banyan Tree by Matrimandir?

If you were to ask me, 'What are the two most sacred trees in the world today?' I would answer without hesitation, 'The Service Tree over the Samadhi of Sri Aurobindo and the Mother and the Banyan Tree at the centre of Auroville'. Mother gave me the work of caring for the Service Tree for the rest of my life. It is an inestimable blessing carrying with it a great responsibility, and it is in this light and with the same sense of devotion that I speak of the Banyan Tree.

Recently you expressed concern about the Banyan.

Yes. Firstly there is the matter of size. One must keep in mind the proportion of the Banyan to the Matrimandir and the perspective and balance of the entire area. We measured the tree the other day and its diameter is now fifty metres, an increase of thirty metres in twenty-eight years! The eastern side of the tree is now at the edge of one of the western petals. It is not difficult to calculate what could happen if this rate of growth is allowed to continue. Then there is the problem of the grass under the Banyan. It is certainly attractive but it has led to serious problems; for example, frequent watering may have contributed to the fungal condition now in the central trunk. Also, the first rule in tree culture is to water deeply but infrequently to encourage the roots to move down into the earth so that they can eventually find their own sources of water. Trees are not at all averse to keeping their roots at ground level or slightly below to take advantage of free water at the surface. This is why they often go into shock when someone who has been watering the grass goes on vacation or forgets to water or an irrigation system breaks down.

The Banyan is a strong tree and can survive long periods of drought. But when it has been force-fed for years things become a lot more precarious. I would not recommend removing the grass immediately, except perhaps for the inner area around the main trunk, but suggest that the interval between watering is gradually extended until the minimum amount of water needed to keep the grass alive is determined. At this point a decision can be made as to whether to continue with minimal watering and keep the grass or remove it completely. I would recommend removal.

As for the aerial roots, I would not recommend that further roots be encouraged to descend without serious study of the necessity of such roots for the support of essential branches. One has only to see the size.

21 May 2005

Note re Matrimandir Gardens:
I. Permanent features of the 12 Matrimandir Gardens

The 12 Matrimandir Gardens may be designed by 12 different landscapers. The unity of the projects will be assured by the fact that each project must be in harmony with its environment, which includes the Matrimandir, the shapes and colour of the 12 petals of the meditation rooms and of the 12 counter petals, the lay-out of the pathways, and the design of the crests as they are defined below.

A. Pathways
1. The layout of the 12 radial pathways from the Matrimandir up to the Oval Road cannot be modified.
2. The width (4.1 metres or 2 metres) cannot be modified.
3. The rainwater gutters on both sides are either 30 cm wide (large pathways) or 25 cm wide (small pathways) with a depth varying from 20 cm (on Matrimandir side) to 23 cm (on the Oval Road side).
4. The pathways are paved with red Agra stones in the middle (140 cm for the wide pathways and 70 cm for the small pathways) and granite stones on both sides, including the rainwater gutters.
5. Each Garden is crossed by a circular pathway. A 2-metre

pathway with Agra and granite stones and gutter is maintained for a minimum of 5 metres on both sides.

B. Areas inside the pathways

In each Garden there is **an area "Petal"** (towards the Matrimandir) and **an area "Garden"** towards the Oval Road. Both areas must remain distinct and not become one area. But they must be also linked.

The area Garden has a well defined **crest** which should be clearly visible and not absorbed in the concept. The forms on the ground have to "dress" the shapes but not kill them.

The **outer slope** of the outer area of each of the 12 Gardens will be covered by grass and is not open for landscaping.

II. Recommendations for the concepts
A. General considerations

1. The concept must take into account that on one side there is an adjacent big Petal continued by the Matrimandir sphere and on the other side there is a lake.
2. In each Garden, the **divisive line** between its area "Petal" and its area "Garden" should not disappear. But that line may take another shape than a classical pathway with Agra and granite.
3. There should not be too much **symmetry**, nor too many **linear** arrangements.
4. Emphasis may be put on the **movement** of the concept.
5. The **main element of the concept, its strong point,** must be highlighted and put in relief. Other elements should not compete or distract the attention.
6. Globally, the areas of the Gardens must **not be overcrowded**.

7. The concept for one specific Garden must also take into account that this Garden is not a unique and outstanding **piece of art**. Eleven other Gardens will be integrated.
8. **Elements sculptural** should be rather more evocative than descriptive.
9. Most of the elements in the Garden must be **flexible and mobile**.
10. **Simplicity** may be always in the background of developments.

B. Flowers and plants

1. Few **flowers**. Their presence may be exquisite and the areas reserved for them may not be big.

2. The **hibiscus plants,** with flowers which are often blooming daily, are among the main residents of the Garden and may be one important focus. Other flowers are accompanying. But on the other end, hibiscus' are not the finality of the Gardens. They contribute to express a state of consciousness.

3. For the flowers it is recommended to peruse a list of some 1,000 flowers which are found in the book "The significance of flowers". The flowers have received names from the Mother according to the vibration and the inner truth that she has perceived while being in some inner contact with them.

4. Some **trees** such as palm trees or other medium sized trees may be considered near the oval pathway. They should not hide the view of the Matrimandir for Aurovilians standing behind the lake.

III. Recommendations for the preparation of the 5 mm/m model

1. The **colours** of the various elements in the Garden should receive special attention.
2. The presence and location of each hibiscus and other **flowers** should be clearly shown on the model (one hibiscus will be represented by a 2 cm square).
3. A hibiscus flower (around 10 cm diameter) will occupy an area of ½ mm on such a model, that is one dot. Therefore, it should be noted that hibiscus will highly contribute to the greenery of the garden.
4. In each model, there should be some **strollers** inside the model if they are allowed to walk, or outside if nobody is supposed to enter. Benches and people sitting on them have to be shown if benches are there.
5. The night element should also be outlined.

IV. Recommendations for the prototypes

A concept may be retained by the Panel either as a project to be executed immediately or as a prototype to be experimented with.

The purpose of a prototype is to get an appraisal of the shapes, the volumes, the colours, the positions of the flowers with cheap materials. For that purpose, a budget is given to develop the concept with, as far as possible, waste or substitute cheap materials. When the budget is spent, the Panel decides if the experiment is to be stopped or pursued or transformed into a final project.

The 12 States of Consciousness
  Existence (Sat)
  Consciousness (Chit)
  Bliss (Ananda)
  Light
  Life
  Power
  Wealth
  Usefulness
  Progress
  Youth
  Harmony
  Perfection

1 June 2005

Dirk Nagelschmidt wrote:

Dear Kireet,

I like also to see trees in the Gardens, but I think Roger had a totally different taste to you and I and the other Aurovilians and MM Coordinators, who love to see trees in the Gardens. His style is more open, the rare trees are more sculptured.

Therefore I like to forward your question to Narad. Narad, what do you think about it?

See you soon

Dirk

11 June 2005

Kireet wrote to the MM Coordinators giving a plea for trees in Matrimandir Gardens:

Dear Roger,

Today (May 31) Leonard presented his concept for Unity Gardens under the Banyan.

I don't want to discuss the design, except the lack of trees in the design.

Not completely true, a tree was there: the Indian almond (*Terminalia catappa*), a fascinating tree with beautiful leaf coloration. Mother called it "Spiritual Aspiration", but it was cut off to soar to heaven after the first layer of branches. Nowadays trees are taken out in Matrimandir area without replacing them or the hope of replacing them by other trees.

Roger, we would like to know: "Why don't you want trees in Matrimandir Gardens?"

It is hot now at this time of the year, and as a gardener it doesn't make sense to me to create gardens without trees. Trees will be the skeleton in the Gardens. I have been writing indirectly about the need to have trees in the Gardens; I don't need to repeat it again.

We can agree to leave views in the direction of Matrimandir between the trees. The Park is too much forest-like and for a park the trees are too close together. But then we were not allowed to create The Park and many years of neglect has done no good. Beautiful trees, pruned in a proper way, will give the area a majestic grandeur.

Trees will not degrade the beauty of Matrimandir, they will enhance it, as they will beautify the Gardens as well.

With all my respect for you as the architect of Matrimandir I ask you to give us Aurovilians trees in Matrimandir Gardens, as I am sure that most Aurovilians will agree that trees are an essential asset of the Gardens.

Any gardener or landscaper will include trees, unless you tell them not to do so.

You can invite landscapers from outside and for sure they will say that trees will be part of a garden like Matrimandir Gardens, unless you tell them you don't want trees.

But Matrimandir Gardens without trees will not be a garden.

Hopefully,
Kireet

undated

To Dr. Hanna from Michael Tait:

Dear Dr Hanna,

Richard Eggenberger has shared with us his great pleasure at meeting with you in April and has given to us a brief appreciation of your considerable achievements at the University of Georgia.

We should like to express our gratitude to you for making available to Richard the turf samples. With these we hope to dramatically reduce our water requirements whilst retaining the beauty of year round grass cover.

To have available to us through Richard the facility of your advice and your expertise is indeed a grace.

With many thanks from the Matrimandir Team
Michael

undated, but approx 2005

Reflections on the Matrimandir Gardens by Narad:
For some months now I have felt a deep and genuine sincerity in some who have come to help manifest the Matrimandir Gardens, bringing with them a knowledge of landscape design as well as a love of Nature and an aspiration to learn the culture of tropical plants, especially those Mother has chosen to represent each Garden. Many of these dedicated workers are also fully aware of the aim of Auroville and the Integral Yoga of the Mother and Sri Aurobindo. Some aspire to learn the spiritual significances Mother has given to the flowers, and to participate in the physical work so essential to the maintenance of gardens, especially under these challenging climatic conditions. To these workers, gardeners, architects, and facilitators, I offer all my help.

The words that Mother spoke to me more than 35 years ago reverberate constantly in my soul, and I know that in the course of time the Matrimandir Gardens will be realised according to the Divine Will. In what time frame this will occur depends a little on us. For we are not here merely to create beautiful gardens – that can be and is accomplished today by professionals all over the world. With unlimited budgets, magnificent botanical gardens, golf courses, parks, public and private gardens are designed, created and maintained and are of such splendour that they uplift and inspire all who enter. It has been a special blessing that I have been able to see many of these, including the great gardens of Japan.

The Matrimandir Gardens are building us, and years after Mother spoke to me of them we are still striving to find the harmony and develop the trust and goodwill to work with each other in a spirit of true collaboration. I believe that we are aspiring for and realizing this more and more. The Gardens will be unlike anything yet seen by man, for each Garden will radiate a state of consciousness according to its significance, a force field so powerful that when one enters one will immediately experience the significance of that Garden.

I will not voice a strong opposition to the suggestion of inviting outside architects to submit designs, for perhaps among them a few will have heard of the Mother and Sri Aurobindo and be open to the ideals and aspiration of Auroville; some may even have an idea of the spiritual significances flowers contain, but I would ask, is it not enough to begin with the many souls in Auroville who have expressed an aspiration to participate in designing the Gardens?

When I sent Mother my letter of 10 February 1973 telling Her that I was empty of all ideas and wished to serve in the new way, I received the following letter from Shyam Sunder.

> "Narad,
> I have read your letter of 10*th* to Mother.
> Mother says that the Matrimandir gardens' execution has been already told in detail to Roger. That is what is to be done.
> Shyam Sunder"

When Roger comes this year it would be a true blessing for all of Auroville and especially the Matrimandir Gardens team if he would share with us exactly what Mother told him, as

Her words are so clear in Shyam Sunder's reply. It would give all of us a deeper understanding of what must be done. As I have said in the past, I will work with Roger in harmony and in a true spirit of collaboration as with all who wish to realise the Gardens. Now that I am staying longer each year I can offer assistance and share the innumerable blessings Mother has given me through the inner contact with the world of plants and on the physical plane of propagating, planting and maintaining them.

On a practical level I am meeting with a number of Aurovilians who are working for the Gardens, and some major steps have already been taken towards the acquisition of equipment and tools, expanding the work of composting, soil testing, the recent introduction of new grasses and groundcovers, discussions of additional plant selections for specific gardens, cultural requirements such as soil preparation, soil amendments, turf management, in depth discussions of the spiritual significances Mother has given to flowers, preliminary colour palettes, addressing the role of trees, techniques of pruning, shaping plants to a greater level of beauty to be fit for inclusion in the Gardens, grafting the more delicate varieties of hibiscus Mother chose for some of the Gardens on strong rootstock to enable them to withstand the intense heat, addressing water requirements, controlling desiccating winds, and more.

We are now in the process of identifying and evaluating equipment and tools available in India, and have begun importing key items from abroad. With the kind and generous assistance of officials in the government of India we will receive, on request, permits to import plants such as water lilies and other aquatic species for the Garden of Wealth and new plants of exceptional merit to add to the beauty of the Matrimandir Gardens.

Planting sods of earth & grass near the Matrimandir

My next visit to India is planned from mid November to the first of March, during which time I will always be available to assist those who truly aspire to realise the Gardens of the Matrimandir.

Narad

undated

Note from Narad
We are not building the Matrimandir, the Matrimandir is building us.
 Narad
 In 1961 Mother invited me to come to the Ashram with Her words to Jyotipriya, "He may come and stay as long as he likes". She accepted me as an Ashramite and I was given 'Prosperity', began an Ashram Choir that sang to Mother on

Christmas Eve, and received innumerable blessings from Her and Sri Aurobindo.

In 1968 She invited me to come for the inauguration of Auroville, and when I met Her, She said, "You don't want to come to Auroville in a few years? I feel you can do something there". So I have had the special honour of Her choosing me to be an Ashramite and an Aurovilian. The programme of recent years is that I live and work with the Ashram students teaching music in the Ashram and help build the Matrimandir Gardens.

As one can feel the sanctity of the Ashram and the Presence of Mother and Sri Aurobindo pervading the very air, one can feel too the powerful force of the New World at work in the earth of Auroville and in Aurovilians. There are many great points of light such as Savitri Bhavan and the great force-field of the Matrimandir, whose rays spread throughout the world and touch all who are open. All of Auroville and especially the Matrimandir and Savitri Bhavan are generating stations of the higher consciousness, inviting all to an "Adventure of Consciousness and Joy" and the New World that is born.

As the next phase of the Matrimandir Gardens begins this year I would like to look back a moment and reflect upon the history and evolution of the Gardens and all that I received directly from Mother. Although I feel within that the Gardens are already built and only wait the opportunity for our openness and collective harmony to descend, there is much to do on the physical level as well as the inner work on ourselves. A deeper knowledge of the spiritual significances of the flowers is the best beginning along with karma yoga.

The following is an address I gave to Aurovilians and the workers in the Matrimandir Gardens and a subsequent update, both published in the journal 'Collaboration'.

28 July 2005

Narad addresses the Matrimandir Gardens workers:

Tomorrow is my birthday, and I feel it is of deep significance to be with you today. I have asked for this meeting to share some of the experiences of my darshans of Mother, the blessings She has showered upon me, the work She has given me, and something of my life with this magical world of plants and flowers as well as my work in the years since 1981 when I left Auroville. I requested Sanjeev to join us as I feel very strongly that Mother has sent him to help implement the work of the gardens. He will facilitate imports of plants and equipment and already has taken on some of the mantle of Madanlal in seeing that funds flow into the Matrimandir. It is a privilege and a blessing to have him work with us. When I arrived on the 21st of this month Sanjeev had already arranged with Customs officials to allow the grass to come in without permits, quarantine, etc. Sanjeev has further arranged for me to meet Mr. A.K. Singh this Saturday evening.

Group of Matrimandir Gardens workers, with Lieske (7th from left), Alan Klass (6 further places to right, at back) and Mary Helen (5th from right)

Doraikannan

I would like to tell you now of some of my extraordinary experiences with Mother, for many of us feel that another moment has come for the Matrimandir Gardens to be realised. These are my most sacred reminiscences. I begin with some autobiographical notes.

My first experience with flowers was approximately at the age of 5. It was a wonderful awakening to beauty. My mother had planted hyacinths (Pride of Beauty) in flower beds around the house. When I saw them my child's heart leapt with joy and immediately I went and pulled off the flowers and ran to my mother with the bouquet. Today I can still see the mixture of pain and happiness in her face on seeing her child bring her flowers and knowing that her flower beds had been destroyed.

At the age of eleven I began cutting lawns in our neighbourhood, pushing a lawn mower (a true push mower as there were no motorized mowers in the late 1940's!) two miles to cut various lawns. My father changed professions when I was still in my early teens and became partners with a landscaper. This was to change my life as well, as I worked for him all through my teenage years and during the summers when I was in college. We designed landscapes and maintained properties, installed new lawns, renovated old ones, pruned trees, and started a plant nursery at a new home on 3 acres, where I learned the value of compost, soil pH and also began to study the bio-dynamic methods of Rudolf Steiner.

When I was 17 it was discovered that I had an operatic voice. I began voice lessons in New York City with Rosalie Miller, the teacher of many opera stars, and was given a four-year scholarship by the famous mezzo-soprano, Regina Resnik, to study for the Metropolitan opera. At the same time I was guided from within to study Raja Yoga with a Pandit in New York City. He promised me a scholarship to Shantiniketan to continue my music studies. I followed him to California but he did not keep his word, and told me that if I really wanted to do yoga I should return to my family and practice calm. In a voice that I hardly recognize today as my own I said, "No, I am going to India!" I had just turned twenty three.

Within a day or two I met Jyotipriya, whose name had been given to her by Sri Aurobindo, when as a young woman she came alone to India to find the secret of the Veda. Jyoti told me about Mother, and said that she would send my photo and a sample of my handwriting to Her. Incredibly, within days Mother sent Her reply: "Tell him he may come and stay as long as he likes". So I was accepted in the Ashram, given Prosperity, joined in athletics, and even formed a choir that sang to Mother on Christmas Eve. But that is a story already published. The tale of my harrowing journey to India to kneel at the feet of the Mother cannot be told here, but during my meeting with Her, lasting about one hour, She said to me, "You must bring down a new music".

I said, "But Mother I don't know anything about combining words and music".

Mother said, "No, no, you must go far above words and bring down the pure music".

I have concentrated on this for the past 44 years, and now the music is coming through the OM Choirs started by Her Grace in the Ashram and Auroville. I invite all who aspire for the descent of the new music and the new world to join us.

I did not stay long in the Ashram as my vital was too restless, returning to the U.S. in 1962. Before returning Mother wrote to me: "Go on boldly, following your way with joy and confidence, taking great care of one thing only, never to forget the Divine". She also wrote: "Keep living in you the spirit of consecration and all will be alright". During my time in the Ashram Mother gave me permission to teach music in the Sri Aurobindo International Centre of Education, wrote answers to my questions, sent me food to supplement my dining room food, and gave me experiences that I cannot even begin to speak of all these years later. When She saw me before leaving She remembered everything in my last letter to Her, and point by point elaborated in detail on her written answers to me.

When I returned to the U.S. I worked at different jobs to put food on the table, married Anie, and did whatever I could for the Ashram, including taking up the work of handmade watercolour paper which I asked Mother to name. She gave the name, 'Arvind'. I made contacts with the most well-known watercolour artists in the U.S., who wrote glowing assessments of the Arvind watercolour paper. Through all these years Mother sent me beautiful birthday cards and blessed my life continually.

One winter during the mid 1960's, I was delivering organic bread to New York City from Connecticut. We were descending a steep hill in a blizzard and the roads were filled with ice. Two ladies had stalled their car perpendicular to traffic. There was no way to stop or to miss them and we crashed into them. Anie's head went into the windshield and she required many stitches. Mother was informed and said that she would have no scars. An Ashramite also saw Mother standing at the foot of Anie's bed in the hospital. We recovered $3,000 in damages and I wrote to Mother immediately saying that I wanted to send the money to Her.

Mother replied: "Why don't you use the money to come for the inauguration of Auroville". We purchased two tickets (exactly $3,000) and came to the Ashram. There were three of us, Isadore from the East-West Cultural Center, Anie and myself. We knelt at Mother's feet and She first looked at Isadore for a brief moment and then turned to Anie and said: "This is not the first time we have met. You have been with me many times before, many, many times". Then Mother turned to me and said: "You don't want to come to Auroville in a few years? I feel you can do something there". I replied, "Yes, Mother, whatever is Your Will". Mother gave me permission to photograph the Inauguration and the many rolls of slides I took are part of Auroville's collection.

We returned to the U.S. in March 1968, and I managed one restaurant and then was a partner in another. This was a period when I made a lot of money. Yet, a day came when I began to hear a voice within saying, "Go to California and help Jyotipriya". I wrote Mother but received no answer, and after a month wrote to Her again saying that the guidance to go to help Jyotipriya had not stopped. Mother sent a telegram saying, "My answer to you was so positive that I thought I had written it!" So I gave up my restaurant business and we left for California to assist Jyotipriya at the East-West Cultural Center. To have some income I found employment in the finest Garden Centre in Beverly Hills, answering such questions from Hollywood stars as "Which end of a tuberous begonia is up?" The garden centre was a very profitable enterprise, and the owner had taken a deep liking to me. As he had no family left he called me into his office one day and said that he considered me his son and wanted to give me the business as he was getting too old to manage. Would I consider it?

It was not to be three years until Mother called me to Auroville, however, for one day I received a letter from Udar. He wrote: "Mother asked me to write you and tell you that She wants you to prepare to come and build the Gardens of the Matrimandir". Joy and my gratitude filled my heart! I replied to Udar asking if Mother wanted me to attend formal classes in college or engage in practical work. Mother replied that the best would be a combination of both. So, I prepared to work for three years and took courses at the University of California, Los Angeles, in Plant Combination Theory, toured some of the finest landscapes in this wealthy area of California with well-known architects, and studied sub-tropical plant life, for until now all my experience had been with temperate climate species. How subtly Mother works! Moving to California introduced me to a wide range of plants closer to the climate of Auroville. I never would have been exposed to these species had we remained in New York.

So, I thought I had three years to prepare, and in only nine months I received the briefest note from Mother, "A bientot" (see you soon).

Anie came first and we were given a place at Promesse. After settling all our affairs I came in December 1969 and we met Mother again. I believe it was on Anie's birthday, December 18. It was at this time that Mother spoke these words about the Gardens that you all have read. Mother's voice was so strong, so clear. She said, "It must be a thing of great beauty, of such a beauty that when men enter they will say, 'Ah, this is it,' and they will experience physically and concretely, the significance of each Garden. In the Garden of Youth they will know youth. In the Garden of Bliss they will know bliss, and so on. One must know how to move from consciousness to consciousness". As she said the last sentence Mother moved her hand in an ascending spiral. Anie remembered one additional sentence of Mother: "It (the Gardens) must manifest something of that which we are trying to bring down". Mother also said to me: "You will make some sketches and then show them to me and we will see together". In the Agenda you will see that Mother mentions two young Americans and says something to the effect that I have studied landscape design and we would be coming soon to build the Gardens. At another time Mother said to me, "I would like you to begin with the Garden of Unity".

I was thirty-one years old. I met with Pierre (Le Grand) at Promesse, for though I have a deep love of art, I can't even draw a crooked line. Pierre made some drawings as I received inspiration, but I never got to show them to Mother. Also, since this was early 1970, the Matrimandir construction had not even begun. I did have certain powerful experiences during this time and have written some of them down. Recently Anie sent me a dream-experience she sent to Mother and to which Mother replied in Her own hand. I do not remember the entire sequence but I saw a golden tree in the sky, more beautiful than anything on earth, and I said, "I must bring a branch of this down to earth and plant it for Mother". I began to climb into the sky and people on the earth below were concerned that I would fall. I had no fear, however, for I was determined to transplant this golden tree on earth, in Mother's garden. I finally was able to reach a branch and brought it down. Mother wrote: "It is not quite a dream and it is a very good indication of the work you are doing".

Thus began a period of twelve years in Auroville in which I was guided to prepare a nursery to introduce, acclimatize and study hundreds of species of ornamental shrubs, trees, vines and ground covers, to determine if they were of sufficient beauty to be introduced into the Matrimandir Gardens. The first task was to find an appropriate site for a nursery as close to the area that would be the Matrimandir in the place called 'Peace'.

I found the best possible location, one that was protected in the west by a canyon, on the south by a lower road, and on the north by a wadi, although the whole area would require fencing. At the same time Amrit went separately and chose the same location. Mother gave Her blessings, and we began.

There were a number of mango trees that provided shade for delicate seedlings and helped to break the wind. You cannot know how difficult it was in those days, when a month's work under the most trying conditions could be wiped out in an hour by a herd of goats or cattle. The goatherds purposely sent their animals in to graze. But enough of those stories, there are too many to relate! Around this time Mother also gave me the incomparable blessing to be the first to read Savitri in Auroville. I read each week for more than ten years.

Anie left Auroville to return to the U.S. in 1971, and Mary Helen and I began a collaboration of 31 years until her passing in 2002. All through the 1970's we travelled the length and breadth of India, occasionally accompanied by Alan Klass who devoted himself to building the orchid section. Each year on Mother's birthday we held a Flower Show. Ashramites and Aurovilians all participated. Pottery sections made beautiful vases, others skilled in the art of calligraphy made cards with Mother's significance and the botanical name, and everyone brought flowers. One year we had nearly 400 flower significances on display. Buses were arranged from the Ashram and hundreds of Ashramites walked with Aurovilians through the Matrimandir Nursery. We also had music, with Alan's classical guitar waking us early in the morning. Each Wednesday we had a classical music evening in our home. Mary Helen's mother donated a stereo system, and we brought hundreds of records to share and many Aurovilians attended through the years.

Mary Helen and I made a world tour of botanical gardens in 1977 to collect the best species and hybrids of trees and shrubs for the Matrimandir Gardens. Wherever we went, all doors were open to us. No one ever refused to help with the Gardens. We reached Singapore so overloaded that the people looked at us with incredulity. Somehow we were able to contact Devan Nair, Mother's disciple, and, I believe, President of Singapore at the time, and he had everything sent through without any duty!

During the 1970's we compiled an Index Seminum, and thus began years of seed exchanges with more than 60 botanical gardens in 30 countries. Today this collaboration continues. On a visit to Florida two years ago people offered more plants than I could carry. There were wonderful trees and shrubs, many exquisitely fragrant, now growing at the Lake to be propagated when we are ready with the Matrimandir Gardens. A friend brought the whole group of plants to Thailand, then another friend carried them from Thailand to India and brought them to me at the Ashram. I recently was given the three varieties of the finest turf produced in thirty-five years of research by Dr. Wayne Hanna of the Agricultural Experimental Station in Tifton, Georgia, a southern area of Georgia known for its intense heat and humidity! These grasses are now being grown in trial plots in the Matrimandir Gardens area. This year I also brought new varieties of lotuses and water lilies. They too have been planted at the Lake and as soon as the Garden of Wealth is ready we will have these beautiful plants available for the ponds.

When I began planting hundreds of trees in the 'Outer Gardens', now known as 'The Park', I did so in accordance with Roger's plans. Vikas held the plans and showed me exactly where to plant. As there was much construction during the late 1970's and early 1980's I could only plant in the west and south quadrants. My aspiration was to plant trees whose flowers, foliage or bark represented that aspect of the Divine Mother: in the west, Mahasaraswati and in the south, Maheshwari. The species from tropical Australia and South America flourished and were the greatest successes, but many others from tropical climates also adapted well. We corresponded with the Royal Botanic Garden in Scotland and the Royal Horticultural Society in England, went on collecting trips with the Chief Conservators of Forests in India, and shared our seeds and our experiences with all. Today in the Park there are magnificent trees found nowhere else in India, growing alongside the many indigenous varieties we also planted. It is a great botanical collection, and I pray that it will be cared for with the highest consciousness. Botanists such as Father Matthew have come at the request of Walter at Shakti and have identified many of the species, as all the original data had been lost. I would add one last comment about 'The Park' in appreciation of the work by the young men from the Ashram who often came in buses at midnight to dig pits for the trees. Without their help much less would have been achieved, as the work, as anyone who has dug holes in Auroville will attest, was strenuous and exhausting. Perhaps I can add one anecdote. Often the boys who were digging the pits would have some fun and put a group of lanterns together to watch the coming show. First a line of ants would form, then the frogs would come to feast on the ants, then the small owls would come and eat the small frogs, and finally the huge white owls would descend for a grand feast.

In the early 1970's, after a cyclone had broken a huge limb of the Service tree and I helped the young men of the Ashram make a proper cut, Mother sent me a blessings packet through Parichand, the Ashram gardener and my elder brother, to care for the Service tree for the rest of my life. Every time I have worked on the Service tree I have experienced Darshan. It is at once a supreme grace and a great responsibility, as is the care of the Banyan at the centre of Auroville, also given to my care along with the Matrimandir Gardens. We have the extraordinary blessing of living near the two most sacred trees on earth, the Service tree and the Banyan. When I left Auroville in 1981, believing I would be gone for only a few months, I saw Nolini one last time. He blessed me and asked me only one question, "Who will take care of the Service Tree?" I promised that I would return to see to its care, and now the Divine has brought me back to assist in building the Matrimandir Gardens once again.

During the early 1970's, Richard Pearson and I met three times a week in the Ashram laboratory and made the first botanical revision of the book of Mother's flower significances, 'Flowers and Their Messages'. Then, together with Mary Helen and Mary Aldridge, we revised the text. During 2000-2001 Mary Helen and I did another complete revision of the botanical section for the two-volume edition of the flower book that Lilo worked on for many years.

From 1970-1972, the last years that Mother was with us for naming flowers, a brief period in which I sent flowers to Her as often as possible, She named more than 60 flowers from the Matrimandir Gardens Nursery. Almost all the rare hibiscus bearing the name Auroville, which Mother later said should also be called the New Creation to expand the scope of the significance, came from Hawaii originally. They were acquired by the Lal Bagh Gardens in Bangalore, with whom we had a wonderful collaboration, and shared with us. In addition to the hibiscus Mother gave many luminous and powerful significances to flowers grown in the Matrimandir Nursery. Here are a few. Remembrance of Sri Aurobindo, Opening to Sri Aurobindo's Force, To Live Only for the Divine. A friend recalls that the last flower I sent to Her before She said, in late 1972, "The time for naming flowers is over", is from the trees where Matrimandir workers now park their cycles and motorcycles, the flowers of *Pterospermum acerifolium* Mother named Realisation of the Supramental Riches.

Making pots, which are still in use in the Lal Bagh Gardens in Bengalaru

The Matrimandir Gardens Nursery is a sacred place, blessed by the Mother. Its only purpose, however, is to introduce, acclimatize, evaluate and produce the finest plants for the Matrimandir Gardens. After walking through it the past few years I could hardly find any shrubs or hibiscus that were of a high enough quality for the Gardens. The work of the Nursery is a full time labour and must be attended to as one's Sadhana, as is the constant labour of pruning, fertilizing, and maintaining trees in the Park.

During the 1980's and throughout the 1990's, after we had left Auroville, with no prospect of work, Chali of high school age and only $400 to our name, Mother opened every door for me. I had written a thesis on Plumeria, Psychological Perfection, and corresponded with the founder of the Plumeria Society of America. In only a few days after arriving in Houston, Texas, to address the Plumeria Society, I was offered a position where I continued my work and my studies of plants, especially sub-tropicals (as Houston is not at all unlike Auroville for five months of the year), owning and operating retail nurseries, building a major composting facility in Texas with two partners, formulating specialty soil mixes as Vice-President of Marketing, and finally moving to Georgia, where Mary Helen and I created our labour of love, a garden with more than 1,200 varieties where month after month Nature reveals a breathtaking pageant of beauty. During this time we also built a successful mail order business in tropical plants, produced a major tropical plant catalogue and published two books, one on Oleanders and one on Plumerias.

In the past seven years I feel some very positive things have been accomplished. I received the permission of the Ashram Trust to develop a website exclusively devoted to Sri Aurobindo's epic poem, Savitri. The URL is www.savitribysriaurobindo.com. It was completed on Sri Aurobindo's birthday in the year 2000, and with the help of Laxmikant Rashinkar, a disciple of Mother and Sri Aurobindo and a computer expert, we are constantly adding new material. Soon LK, as he is known, will complete a major search engine on the site so that any word, term or line in Savitri can be found almost instantaneously. Currently the Savitri website contains the complete text of the poem, Sri Aurobindo's letters on the poem, an extensive section of Mother's words on Savitri, another section of Her reciting Savitri, a biography of Sri Aurobindo, and more. When the website was completed I began another work on Savitri, a major opus entitled 'Lexicon of an Infinite Mind', a dictionary of words and terms in Savitri. All through the years of Mary Helen's heroic battle with cancer we worked many hours a day to complete the book. Dr. Alok Pandey offered to proof read the manuscript, which has now been published.

Another work begun during this time is a book on the Service tree, a homage containing the history of the tree, recollections, poems, paintings and photographs through the seventy-five years since its planting. The past two years have also occupied much time in developing a Lending Library of CD's of classical music, both Indian and Western, in the Ashram (shared with Kamel who is in charge of the library in Auroville), and a DVD Library of great motion pictures, musical performances, ballet, art, history, science, and more. These are being shared with Claude, who is in charge of the DVD collection in Auroville. In November I will continue voice lessons in the Ashram and perhaps prepare another performance with the students for Mother's birthday. We are just beginning work on a new book of Mother's flower significances. This will be titled; 'The Mother's Flower Significances, A Guide to Identification', and will include a photograph of every flower named by Mother. As often as is possible the flower will be shown in its exact size, in full and accurate colour, with the Mother's significance, botanical name and Her commentary. The outer edge of the pages will be the colour of the rainbow. If one has a blue flower one turns to the blue section to see all the blue flowers Mother named, graded from tiny to very large. The book will be printed on thin but strong paper and will be priced very reasonably. Lastly, I have just signed a contract for a book entitled 'Flowers for the Soul', to be published in the U.S., with all proceeds to be divided between two Sri Aurobindo Centres, Matagiri in New York and Sri Aurobindo Sadhana Peetham in California, as I am presently involved in helping to further the work of both centres. Very dedicated souls have built these centres and maintained them for many years, and we all now feel an impetus to expand and embrace those who are seeking the Life Divine. I have asked Mother for guidance, and one word keeps coming to me, "Prepare". I am also continuing my studies of Savitri.

I have been supremely blessed by the Divine Mother to have lived a life among plants and flowers, in the uplifting atmosphere of music, art, literature and poetry, and now to be among you to help realise the Gardens of the Matrimandir.

Before I close I would like to touch on some practical matters. I have discussed some of these with Kireet and others who understand the need for essential equipment, and well-made tools. Those who have worked intimately with the earth, lived in Nature's realms of beauty, shared her offerings, collaborated with her in further beautification, can perhaps be a little aware of the enormity of the scale of work before us. Before anything is realised we must have the sub-structure, irrigation, composting facility, soil preparation, proper equipment to move plants and soil, mowing machines, rototillers, power edgers, and proper tools for grading, digging, etc. Then comes the complex challenge of plant selection, the study of plant care, including pruning, shaping, fertilizing, insect and disease control. I will select the best available equipment in India, Europe and the U.S. in collaboration with others, and decide upon those that can be purchased here and those that have to be imported, and through Sanjeev's contacts we hope to acquire them soon.

For many years I lived with a sense of failure, feeling that I could not sufficiently open and be receptive to the vision Mother had entrusted in me – to design and build the Gardens of the Matrimandir. Recently a dear friend in New York has disabused me of this concern, saying that 12 years or 30 years is nothing to realise a work given by Mother as Her Force is behind all our efforts. All feelings of frustration and failure have now dissolved. I am ready and the time has come for us to work together in harmony and love.

Sri Aurobindo wrote in Savitri:

His failure is not failure whom God leads;
Through all the slow mysterious march goes on:
An immutable Power has made this mutable world;
A self-fulfilling transcendence treads man's road;
The driver of the soul upon its path,
It knows its steps, its way is inevitable,
And how shall the end be vain when God is guide?

We must remember that this is not a far-off impersonal God watching our movements, but the ever-present help and guidance of the Mother and Sri Aurobindo to enable us to transform ourselves in order to bring down the new creation. I seek no name or fame, only to fully surrender to the Mother, to be what She wants me to be and to complete the work

She has given to me. I am at the service of the Divine and therefore at the service of all who aspire for the manifestation of the Gardens.

Here is part of a letter from John Harper written in 2002.

Let Us Start With Unity

A Proposal

"When there is full faith and consecration, there comes also a receptivity to the Force which makes one do the right thing and take the right means, and then the circumstances adapt themselves and the result is visible".

Sri Aurobindo, Letters on Yoga, p 670

"They don't know that one must NOT THINK....."

Mother, in conversation with Satprem regarding the Matrimandir... Agenda: 10 January 1970

In the early 1970's the Mother said to Narad, to whom she had given the task of creating the gardens, that he should start his work with the Garden of Unity (close to the Banyan tree).

"I feel that if we can manage, for the moment, to put our plans and conceptions aside, if we could address ourselves simply to the land that is there calling to be made into this Garden of Unity, then little by little we would be led progressively forward.

If we could gather there near the Banyan, in silence, and then place just one stone or plant one flower, all together, then that would be a true beginning to this most needed Garden.

It is the time to be together in silence and to work together.

All who feel that they have something to contribute to the Garden of Unity are called to join their aspirations and to take a first step in this adventure. The way to go forward will surely be shown, step-by-step."

I know that Mother has given us another opportunity to work in harmony for the Gardens and I am grateful for those she has sent to help manifest them. There are two last points I would like to cover briefly. The first is Mary Helen's letter to Mother about beginning a small experiment in constructing a Japanese Garden. Mary Helen asked Mother if the Auroville gardens (she mistakenly wrote Auroville gardens but meant the Matrimandir Gardens as there were no gardens in Auroville in those days) would be in the Japanese style. You have seen Mother's answer. The second point is my letter to Mother about the size of the Gardens. You know how strongly Huta has disagreed with Roger about the size and design of the Gardens since Mother had told her so many things about them. Huta told me that Mother held a handkerchief in Her hand and squeezed it saying (and I paraphrase here), "Do you think I want something like this?" (really small). Huta encouraged me to write to Mother, and I did. Her reply that Roger knows best about the size of the Gardens is clear, and I do not question it. The Gardens will continue to evolve long after Roger and I have discarded these bodies for new ones, but until that time I shall work in harmony with him and with all who aspire to see them manifest. A sincere goodwill and an aspiration for a true collective harmony will enable us to move forward and accomplish this sacred work for the world.

The following quotation from Mother to Nirodbaran was published in the Matrimandir Newsletter: "The completion of the Matrimandir will be coincidental in establishing world peace and harmony".

Laxmi Narayan once asked a saint from the Himalayas what he experienced after a meditation in the Matrimandir chamber. The saint replied: "One day it will save the world".

At the Service of Truth,
Narad

10 September 2005
Meeting of the Matrimandir Gardens Reflection Group

Present: Alain, Aryamani, Jacqueline, Lala, Léonard, Louis, Marc, Nadja, Narad
Guests: Divya, Gnanavel, Peter

A. Unity Garden Prototype

In this concept, the Banyan tree is considered as the Tree of Unity and the 6 plots as extensions, within waves, of the Unity emanated by the Banyan tree. These waves are even extended beyond the mini-amphitheatre.

This concept raised the issue that the area included between the Banyan tree and the mini-amphitheatre is in fact one area and could be called the **Park of Unity,** and the six plots would no longer be called the Garden of Unity.

With this understanding, a majority of participants have been praising the prototype, which had definitely some professional input and was quite beautiful **as an individual entity,** but they felt that it may not fit into the future Park of Unity.

Nobody objected when it was voiced that the shapes of the pots were not respected by the 40 cm high wall, which was competing with the crests.

31 January 2006

Alain G wrote:
　Subject: Rosa's Trust
　Dear Narad,

I told Michael Bonke that he will probably receive a request for reimbursement of expenses done for contouring inside the plots and for grass, on a monthly basis. I understand that you like to add the Nursery expenditure, which I would not do.

　The headings of the recurrent expenses are found in the attached file. Any specific garden equipment could be added after agreement from the trustees.

This request is matching the object of the trust: no financing of pathways nor prototypes but only final gardens. The contours inside the pathways are final and the grass area is final.

I am seeing with Divya to open two new headings: Contour and Grass.

At your disposal for further collaboration on this issue, Alain

date unknown

Narad writes to Alain G

Dear Alain,

We have both spoken frankly and I appreciate that I now understand more of the plan. I have also viewed both Roger's and Paolo's proposals. I can only say, in all honesty, that my opinions and even my inner feelings are worthless. The Lord is building Auroville and He shall work through his instruments for its manifestation. If He has a role for me it will be disclosed. If I am too closed He will find more receptive souls to realise His vision.

In Mother's Love,
Narad

Alain replies:

Dear Narad,
1. Firstly, no trees in the gardens? If only pots with a few plants this then may be a nice architectural presentation, but it is not a garden. You may remember that I sent to you on May 18, 2002, some recollection of our first attempt to start the gardens on 24 November 1972. It is a reminder that the Mother knew exactly what kind of gardens we were supposed to start: the whole layout of the oval was laid with red tiles, plants were only in pots, no trees within the oval, gardens were quite small (according to your appreciation). Unhappily we do not have any tapes of their discussions. The present idea is to avoid fixed plantations in the Matrimandir area in order to give a great mobility. Pots which may be planted in the soil (it will not be seen that the plants are in pots) or pots which are laid on the ground (pots in brass - brass handa - or in wood like wine casks with brass hoops) or in terra cotta, etc.

2. *Or are the "gardens" still very small? Yes, you may find them very small, while Roger will find them with an appropriate dimension. Is it not?*

...and trees are all around the outer gardens area? Not all around. Only in some places since the basic idea is that the Matrimandir is a living part of the city and must be seen from every corner, as much as possible.

As you can understand, there must be shade in such a tropical climate. Maybe they are meant to be visited up to 10 am and after 4.30 pm during half of the year? There is some idea to provide individual sunshade.

3. Is the entire area for the "inner gardens" to be excavated to the necessary depth in order to bring in the sand? Yes, if we like to store all the water which is needed.

4. Is this not also a cost factor that can be considerable? Considerable cost factor: yes, maybe as costly as the discs and the glass inner skin. Main problem may be to find such an amount of a sand which is already rare.

Bien amicalement, Alain

Article in AV Today

(AV Today published interviews with Narad on the Banyan and Outer Gardens in March 2004 (issue # 182) and in March 2007 (issue #217) when he spoke about the varieties of grasses and other plants he was bringing to the Gardens.)

The beginnings of the Matrimandir Gardens Nursery and the Matrimandir Gardens.

"Mother asked me to write you and tell you that She wants you to prepare to come and build the Gardens of the Matrimandir." From a letter from Udar to Narad in 19...??? In this article, Narad reminisces about his life and the starting of the Matrimandir Nursery and Gardens.

I have always had a deep connection to flowers. My first conscious remembrance of dealing with flowers was when, 5 years old, I pulled off the hyacinths my mother had planted in the flower beds around our house and ran to her with the bouquet. Her face was a mixture of pain and happiness, seeing her child bring her flowers and knowing that her flower beds had been destroyed! My connection became deeper when, at about the age of eleven, my father became partner with a landscaper. Throughout my teenage years and afterwards during the summers when I was in college I helped him designing landscapes and maintaining gardens and estates, installing and renovating lawns, pruning trees, and running a plant nursery.

When I was 17, I was guided from within to study Raja Yoga with a Pundit in New York City. I followed him to California where I met Dr. Judith Tyberg, who had been named Jyotipriya by Sri Aurobindo when as a young woman she came to India to find the secret of the Veda.

She spoke with all the great scholars and they agreed that the Vedas were a fable and had no deeper meaning. On her last day a gentleman came to her and presented her with the typewritten manuscript of the 'Secret of the Vedas' by Sri Aurobindo. She read it immediately and knew that she had found her guru and proceeded directly to Pondicherry.

Jyotipriya, who had founded the East-West Cultural Center in Los Angeles in 1953, told me about The Mother and said that she would send Her my photo and a sample of my handwriting. Incredibly, within days Mother sent Her reply: "Tell him he may come and stay as long as he likes". I came in 1961 and was accepted in the Ashram, given Prosperity, joined in athletics, and even formed a choir that sang to Mother on Christmas Eve.

I did not stay long in the Ashram as my vital was too restless. I returned to the U.S. in 1962. Before returning Mother wrote to me: "Go on boldly, following your way with joy and confidence, taking great care of one thing only, never to forget the Divine". She also wrote: "Keep living in you the spirit of consecration and all will be alright". Back in the U.S. I worked at different jobs, married Anie Nunnally, and did whatever I could for the Ashram. Through all these years Mother sent me beautiful birthday cards and blessed my life continually.

One winter during the mid 1960's, Anie and I were delivering organic bread to New York City from Connecticut. We were descending a steep hill in a blizzard and the roads were filled with ice. Two ladies had stalled their car perpendicular to traffic and were "rumbling around to find a flashlight". There was no way to stop or to miss them and we crashed head on into them. Anie's head went into the windshield and she required many stitches. Mother was informed and said that she would have no scars. We recovered $3,000 in damages and I wrote to Mother immediately saying that I wanted to send the money to Her. Mother replied: "Why don't you use the money to come for the inauguration of Auroville." We purchased two tickets (exactly $3,000) and came to the Ashram. We knelt at Mother's feet. When She first turned to Anie She said: "This is not the first time we have met. You have been with me many times before, many, many times". Then Mother turned to me and said: "You don't want to come to Auroville in a few years? I feel you can do something there". I replied, "Yes, Mother, whatever is Your Will". Mother gave me permission to photograph the Inauguration and the many rolls of slides I took are part of Auroville's collection.

We returned to the U.S. in March 1968, and as I thought it would be long before Mother would call me to work for Auroville I started work as a manager of a restaurant and became a partner in another. In this period I made a lot of money. Yet, a day came when I began to hear a voice within saying, "Go to California and help Jyotipriya". I wrote to Mother but received no answer and after a month wrote to

Her again saying that the voice prompting me to go and help Jyotipriya had not stopped. Mother sent a telegram saying, "My answer to you was so positive that I thought I had written it!" I gave up my restaurant business and we left for California to assist Jyotipriya at the East-West Cultural Center. To have some income I found employment in the finest Garden Centre in Beverly Hills, answering such questions from Hollywood stars as "Which end of a tuberous begonia is up?" The garden centre was a very profitable enterprise and the owner had taken a deep liking for me. As he had no family left he called me into his office one day and said that he considered me his son and wanted to give me the business as he was getting too old to manage it. Would I consider it? The business and the property were already worth millions of dollars. But Mother had other plans for me.

One day, around the spring of 1969, I received a letter from Udar. He wrote: "Mother asked me to write you and tell you that She wants you to prepare to come and build the Gardens of the Matrimandir". Joy and gratitude filled my heart! I replied to Udar asking if Mother wanted me to attend formal horticultural classes in college or engage in practical work before coming to Auroville. Mother replied that the best would be a combination of both. I quit my job at the garden centre, found a job with a large landscape design firm, and took courses at the University of California, Los Angeles, in Plant Combination Theory, with a wonderful teacher, Philip Chandler, who befriended me and from whom I learned much. I also took tours of some of the most beautifully landscaped homes in this wealthy area of California, with well-known architects, and studied sub-tropical plant life, for until now all my experience had been with temperate climate species.

How subtly Mother works! Moving to California introduced me to a wide range of plants closer to the climate of Auroville. I never would have been exposed to these species had we remained in New York.

Anie came first to India and Mother gave us rooms at a place called Promesse. After settling all our affairs I came in December 1969 and we met Mother again. I believe it was on Anie's birthday, December 18. It was at this time that Mother spoke these words about the gardens. She said, "It must be a thing of great beauty, of such a beauty that when men enter they will say, 'Ah, this is it,' and they will experience physically and concretely the significance of each garden. In the Garden of Youth they will know youth. In the Garden of Bliss they will know bliss, and so on. One must know how to move from consciousness to consciousness". As she said the last sentence Mother moved her hand in an ascending spiral. Anie remembered one additional sentence of Mother. "It (the Gardens) must manifest something of that which we are trying to bring down". Mother also said to me: "You will make some sketches and then show them to me and we will see together". In the Agenda you will see that Mother mentions two young Americans and says something to the effect that I have studied landscape design and we would be coming soon to build the Gardens. At another time Mother said to me: "I would like you to begin with the Garden of Unity". I was thirty-one years old. The Matrimandir construction had not yet begun.

The founding of the Nursery

Thus began a period of twelve years in Auroville in which I was guided to prepare a nursery to introduce, acclimatize and study hundreds of species of ornamental shrubs, trees, vines and ground covers, to determine if they were of sufficient beauty to be introduced into the Matrimandir Gardens. The first task was to find an appropriate site for a nursery as close to the area that would be the Matrimandir, in the place called 'Peace'.

I found the best possible location, one that was protected in the west by a canyon, on the south by a lower road and on the north by a wadi, although the whole area would require fencing. At the same time Amrit went separately and chose the same location. Mother gave Her blessings and we began. There were a number of mango trees that provided shade for delicate seedlings and helped to break the wind. You cannot know how difficult it was in those days, when a month's work under the most trying conditions could be wiped out in an hour by a herd of goats or cattle. The goatherds purposely sent their animals in to graze. Around this time Mother also gave me the incomparable blessing to be the first to read 'Savitri' in Auroville. I read each week for more than ten years.

From 1970-1972, for a brief period I sent flowers to The Mother which She would name according to their spiritual significance or their 'Message'. She named more than 60 flowers from the Matrimandir Gardens Nursery. Almost all the rare hibiscus bearing the name Auroville, which Mother later said should also be called the *New Creation* to expand the scope of the significance, came from Hawaii originally. They were acquired by the Lal Bagh Gardens in Bangalore, with whom we had a wonderful collaboration of shared plants. In those early days, coming from California and having collected seeds of the most beautiful trees and shrubs, I had heard of the Lal Bagh, a fine Botanical Garden in the city known for the beauty of its trees. In fact, it was known as the Garden City. In addition to giving us the messages of the hibiscus, Mother gave many luminous and powerful significances to flowers grown in the Matrimandir Gardens Nursery. Here are a few. *'Remembrance of Sri Aurobindo', 'Opening to Sri Aurobindo's Force', 'To Live Only for the Divine', 'Joy of Union with the Divine'*, and many more. My dear friend, Tara, recalls that the last flower I sent to Mother before She said, in late 1972, "The time for naming flowers is over", is from the trees where Matrimandir workers now park their cycles and motorcycles, the flowers of *Pterospermum acerifolium* which Mother named 'Realisation of the Supramental Riches'.

During the early 1970's, I met with the Ashram botanist Richard Pearson three times a week in the Ashram laboratory, and made the first botanical revision of the book of Mother's flower significances, *Flowers and Their Messages*. Then, together with Mary Helen and Mary Aldridge, we revised the text. During 2000-2001 Mary Helen and I did another complete revision of the botanical section for the two-volume edition of the flower book that Lilo Burk from the Ashram Archives worked on for many years. [This book was published in 2000 under the title *'The Spiritual Significance of Flowers'*. See AV Today # 133, February 2000.]

In the early 1970's, after a cyclone had broken a huge limb of the Service Tree at Sri Aurobindo's Samadhi, I helped the young men of the Ashram make a proper cut. Mother sent me a blessings packet through my beloved elder brother, Parichand, the Ashram gardener, with Her instructions to care for the Service Tree for the rest of my life. Every time since I have worked on the Service Tree I have experienced Darshan. It is at once a supreme grace and a great responsibility, as is the care of the Banyan at the centre of Auroville, also given to me along with the Matrimandir Gardens. These two trees, the most sacred in all the world, were eventually taken from me, but that is another story.

The Outer Gardens

In the early 1970's, I began planting hundreds of trees in the 'Outer Gardens', now known as 'The Park'. I did so in accordance with Roger Anger's plans. Vikas held the plans and showed me exactly where to plant. As there was much construction during the late 1970's and early 1980's I could only plant in the west and south quadrants. My aspiration was to plant trees whose flowers, foliage or bark represented that aspect of the Divine Mother - in the west, Mahasaraswati and in the south, Maheshwari. The species from tropical Australia and South America flourished and were the greatest successes, but many others from tropical climates also adapted well. We corresponded with the Royal Botanic Garden in Scotland, the Royal Horticultural Society in England, and went on collecting trips with the Chief Conservators of Forests in India and shared our seeds and our experiences with all.

In fact, it was my friendship with the Chief Conservators that led to many trips taken with them into the forests of southern India and my friendship with Dr. Tanikaimani of the French Institute that enabled us to collect many beautiful Vandas in the scrub jungles of Tamil Nadu. Today in the Park there are magnificent trees found nowhere else in India, growing alongside the many indigenous varieties we also planted. It is a great botanical collection, and I pray that it will be cared for with the highest consciousness. Botanists such as Father Matthew (now deceased) have come at the request of Walter at Shakti and have identified many of the species, as all the original data have been lost.

Anie left Auroville to return to the U.S. in 1971. Then Mary Helen and I began a collaboration of 31 years until her passing in 2002. All through the 1970's we travelled the length and breadth of India, occasionally accompanied by Alan Klass who devoted himself to building the orchid section. Each year on Mother's birthday we held a Flower Show. Ashramites and Aurovilians all participated. Pottery sections made beautiful vases, others skilled in the art of calligraphy made cards with Mother's significance and the botanical name of the flower, and everyone brought flowers. One year we had nearly 400 flower significances on display. Buses were arranged from the Ashram and hundreds of Ashramites walked with Aurovilians through the Matrimandir Nursery. I remember the joy of walking with Champaklal and Nirodbaran during the flower show.

(Front row, right to left) Nirodbaran, Champaklal and Narad with others from the Ashram

Mary Helen and I made a world tour of botanical gardens in 1977 to collect the best species and hybrids of trees and shrubs for the Matrimandir Gardens. Wherever we went, all doors were open to us. No one ever refused to help with the Gardens. We reached Singapore so overloaded that the people looked at us with incredulity. Somehow we were able to contact Devan Nair, Mother's disciple, and truly a good friend who was to become the third President of Singapore in 1981 (I am not absolutely certain of the date but think it is correct), and he had everything sent through without any duty! During the 1970's we compiled an Index Seminum and thus began years of seed exchanges with more than 60 botanical gardens in 30 countries.

Back to the USA, and to Auroville again

In 1980 Mary Helen and I and our daughter Chali, who was then of high school age, left Auroville and returned to the USA. This was shortly after the Government of India had promulgated the Auroville Emergency Provisions Act in 1980. We had no prospect of work and only $400. But Mother opened every door. I had written a thesis on *Plumeria*, which Mother had named 'Psychological Perfection', and had corresponded with the founder of the Plumeria Society of America, Elizabeth Thornton. She invited me to address their annual meeting about my experience in growing plumerias in Auroville's climate. In only a few days after arriving in Houston, Texas, to address the Society, I was offered a position where I continued my work and my studies of plants, especially sub-tropicals (as Houston is not at all unlike Auroville for five months of the year), owning and operating retail nurseries, building a major composting facility in Texas with two partners, and formulating specialty soil mixes as Vice-President of Marketing for our firm 'Living Earth Technology'. During this time we also built a successful mail order business in tropical plants, 'The Plumeria People', and 'Tropical Plant Specialists' produced a major tropical plant catalogue and published two books, the first, 'The Handbook on Plumeria Culture', and the second, 'The Handbook on Oleanders'. We moved to Georgia in 1995 where Mary Helen and I created our labour of love, "Mother's Garden", a garden with more than 1,200 varieties where month after month Nature reveals a breathtaking pageant of beauty. But during all these years, the contact with Auroville remained. Chali returned to live in Auroville in 1995, and in 1996 Mary Helen and I returned for a visit celebrating Chali's first child, Dylan. This was the beginning of a renewed contact with Auroville and many visits followed and we resumed work for the Matrimandir Gardens. Today, I spend about five to six months each year in Auroville and six months in the USA.

When I left Auroville in 1981, believing I would be gone for only a few months, I saw Nolini one last time. He blessed me and asked me only one question, "Who will take care of the Service Tree?" I promised that I would return to see to its care. This brought a wide smile from him, and I can't describe how happy I am that the Divine has brought me back to keep my promise and to assist in building the Matrimandir Gardens once again.

Collecting plants for the Matrimandir Gardens continued. On a visit to Florida in 2003 people offered more plants than I could carry. There were wonderful trees and shrubs, many exquisitely fragrant, now growing at the Lake Estate of the Sri Aurobindo Ashram to be propagated when they can be brought to the Matrimandir Gardens. I brought different varieties of the finest turf grasses to Auroville. They were produced over 35 years of research by Dr. Wayne Hanna of the Agricultural Experimental Station in Tifton, Georgia, a southern area of Georgia known for its intense heat and humidity! In 2005 I also brought new varieties of lotuses and water lilies. They too have been planted at the Lake Estate, and as soon as the Garden of Wealth is ready we will have these beautiful plants available for the ponds. Lately, I have brought proper garden equipment to Auroville, such as trommel screens for sieving soils, mowing machines, rototillers, power edgers, and proper tools for grading, digging, and numerous others.

The Matrimandir Gardens Nursery is a sacred place, blessed by the Mother. Its only purpose, however, is to introduce, acclimatize, evaluate and produce the finest plants for the Matrimandir Gardens. The work at the Nursery, the Matrimandir Gardens and the Park is a full time labour and must be attended to as one's sadhana. It is in this spirit that I continue to be involved with the Matrimandir.

Note to Carel, co-editor of AV Today:

Carel,

I would like to add these three sentences just after the next to last paragraph so we can end with the last paragraph and your beautiful ending. During the past four years I have concentrated on collecting warm climate bulbs which Mother has named. I felt these to be of great importance for the future of the Matrimandir Gardens and the surrounding "Park" area. I joined a 'Bulb Society' and brought with me each year dozens of varieties to acclimatize in the Nursery. Among them Crinum *'Disinterested Work Done for the Divine'* and Zephyranthes and Habranthus, *'Prayer'*, which is now one of the largest collections in the world with more than 86 species and hybrids.

Narad

April 2007
On the significances of the twelve Gardens
It must be an expression of that consciousness
which we are trying to bring down. (The Mother)

Research Paper

The aim of this document is to serve as a basis of discussion on what needs to be expressed in each one of the gardens.

Compiled by Gilles G.

The compiler has tried to include faithfully here the comments made in January 2001 by Kireet Joshi to Roger Anger. He has also benefitted from discussions with Narad.

At the centre of Auroville, a *Park of Unity* consisting of twelve gardens

On 23rd June 1965, the Mother told Satprem:

This central point [of Auroville] *is a park I had seen when I was a little girl (perhaps the most beautiful thing in the world with regard to physical, material Nature), a park with water and trees like all parks, and flowers, but not too many (flowers in the form of creepers), palm trees and ferns (all species of palm trees), water (if possible, running water – it must be running water) and, if possible, a small waterfall – running water.*

So in that park I had seen the (...) "Pavilion of the Mother" [Matrimandir]*; but not this* [Mother points to herself]: *the Mother, the true Mother, the principle of the Mother. (I say "Mother" because Sri Aurobindo used the word, otherwise I would have put something else – I would have put "creative principle" or "realising principle" or ... something of that sort.)*

On 25th June 1965, the Mother told Huta:

The Park of Unity will be divided into twelve gardens, which will represent the twelve Attributes of the Supreme Mother.

On 7th September 1965, the Mother wrote a note to Roger:

The Park of Unity must be surrounded by a kind of isolating zone so that it is solitary and silent. One has access to it only with permission

Names given by the Mother to Matrimandir's twelve gardens

On 28th February 1968, during Auroville's inauguration ceremony, one of the many posters exhibited below the banyan tree listed – in French – the names of Matrimandir's 12 gardens:

Existence, Consciousness, Bliss, Light, Life, Power, Wealth, Usefulness, Progress, Youth, Harmony, Perfection.

On the significance of these twelve gardens as a whole

The Mother wrote that: *The Matrimandir wants to be the symbol of the Universal Mother according to Sri Aurobindo's teaching*[1]. Hence Matrimandir and the Mother's symbol symbolise the same thing, which explains why they both represent a lotus in full bloom and why parts of Her symbol and components of the Matrimandir complex/island have the same significance:

Her symbol's centre and Matrimandir itself represent the *Mahashakti* or *Divine consciousness*.

Her symbol's 4 '*petals*' and Matrimandir's 4 pillars represent Her 4 *Aspects* or *Personalities*.

Her symbol's 12 'petals' represent several things:

It signifies anything one wants, you see. Twelve: that's the number of Aditi, of Mahashakti. So it applies to everything; all Her Action has 12 Aspects. There are also Her 12 Virtues, Her 12 Powers, Her 12 Aspects, and then Her 12 Planes of manifestation and many other things that are 12; and the symbol, the number 12 is in itself a symbol. It is the symbol of manifestation, double

---

1 Undated but probably dating from early 1972.

*perfection, in essence and in manifestation, in the creation.*²

*The [Supreme Mother's] twelve attributes.*³

The twelve powers of the Mother manifested for Her work.⁴

Essentially (in general principle) the 12 powers are the vibrations that are necessary for the complete manifestation. *These are the 12 seen from the beginning above the Mother's head*⁵...⁶

Hence, the 12 rooms in Matrimandir's 'petals' seem to represent the Mother's 12 *Virtues* and She told Huta, on 25.06.65, that Matrimandir's 12 gardens would represent the *twelve Attributes of the Supreme Mother*, which is indeed one of the significances She gave of Her symbol's 12 petals (see above). But what does She mean here by *Attributes*? In this case, is it synonymous to *Power*? It is also possible that before naming the 12 gardens (sometime between June 65' and 68'), She decided that they would represent something else than Her 12 *'Attributes'*.

The 12 gardens seem to represent "the twelve powers of the Mother manifested for Her work" and these "are the

---

2 The Mother to Her Wednesday class, 10.11.54.

3. The Mother's handwritten explanation to Huta of the significance of the twelve petals of Her symbol, 02.12.55.

4. The Mother's handwritten explanation of the significance of the twelve petals of Her symbol, 24.01.58. (CWM)

5. While speaking of Tlemcen (Algeria) where She sojourned at the Théons, the Mother said: *"That was where Madame Théon recognised me, because of the formation of* twelve pearls *she saw above my head; and she told me, 'You are that because you have this. Only that can have this!'"* (Mother's Agenda, 11.05.63).

6. Sri Aurobindo's written explanation of the significance of the twelve petals of the Mother's symbol, 15.04.34.

vibrations that are necessary for the complete manifestation". The fact that, out of the 12 flowers the Mother selected as central flower for these 12 gardens, 10 are hibiscus (flowers to which She gave the generic name *Power*) seems to confirm this interpretation.

The Mother's words about Matrimandir gardens to Narad and Anie on 18th December 1969

It must be a thing of great beauty, of such beauty that when people come they will say "Ah, this is it".

One must know how to move from consciousness to consciousness.

It must be an expression of that consciousness which we are trying to bring down.

Narad and Anie also understood that the *Garden of Power* must really express power, the *Garden of Harmony*, harmony, and so forth; that 'the vibration and essence of each garden must be felt.'

The fact that these gardens must *"be an expression of that consciousness which we are trying to bring down"* seems to confirm that these gardens indeed represent the *vibrations that are necessary for the complete manifestation* because, as the manifestation is not yet 'complete', some of these *Powers* need to be conquered and/or *brought down*. This clearly implies that these gardens will evolve with the consciousness of the gardeners – as Roger keeps on saying.

* * *

On a possible grouping of the names of Matrimandir's 12 gardens

Immediately after listing the names of Her twelve *Virtues*, whose names She gave to the 12 rooms in the 'petals', the Mother commented that the first eight were *attitudes towards the Divine* and the last four were *attitudes towards humanity*. Hence we shouldn't be astonished if the names of the twelve gardens can also be grouped in two or more sub-groups.

The first group of 3 gardens is *Sat-Chit-Ananda* (*Existence, Consciousness, Bliss*), which is the essence of the Divine, and, according to Kireet Joshi:

the second group of 3 gardens, *Light, Life, Power* is intimately linked to Chit (Consciousness),

the third group of 3 gardens, *Wealth, Utility, Progress* is intimately linked to Sat (Existence),

the fourth group of three gardens, *Youth, Harmony, Perfection* illustrates *Ananda* (Bliss).

Kireetbhai added:

"Supermind is the whole thing; the Mother is concentrated on the supermind."

"When you realise the psychic, the whole world becomes existent for you".

Existence: psychic.

In *Consciousness*, She speaks of the Supramental.

In *Bliss*, She speaks of Krishna; experience of the intensity which will manifest in the garden.

Divine, Supramental, Psychic are in ALL gardens. There is nothing on the lower levels of consciousness.

* * *

An attempt to understand the sequence in which the Mother listed the twelve gardens

Two things come immediately to mind:

As the list starts with Existence and ends with Perfection, it could be a parable about creation or the present manifestation.

The first six gardens are powers which we humans cannot cultivate, but we should certainly try and cultivate the last six powers.

It does appear that the twelve gardens can be grouped in four groups of three gardens.

First group of three gardens: Existence, Consciousness, Bliss:

'That which has thrown itself out into forms is a triune Existence-Consciousness-Bliss'. (Sri Aurobindo). 'That' in India is called 'Brahman'. All is Brahman. There is nothing that is not Brahman for outside Brahman nothing exists – because all is Brahman. *"There is only That. Only That exists. That, what – Only That exists!"* (The Mother)

Let us note that the Mantra below (which is written twice at Matrimandir's second level) was written in Sanskrit by Sri Aurobindo for the Universal Mother. The first words of its English transliteration were also written by Sri Aurobindo – and the last two by The Mother as he had not written them.

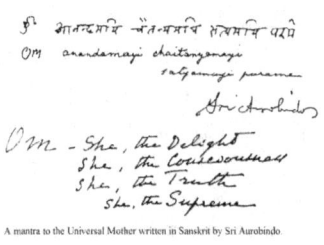

A mantra to the Universal Mother written in Sanskrit by Sri Aurobindo.

The first three words of its English transliteration were also written by Sri Aurobindo - and the last two by The Mother as He had not written them.

Its English translation is by The Mother.

Mother wrote its translation in English and in French. Let us *also note that Existence* and *Truth* are two different words to express the same Reality.

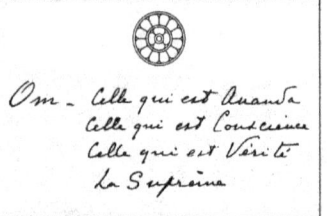 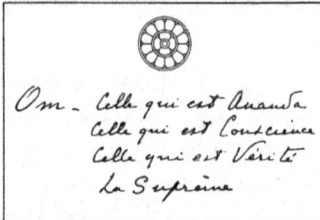

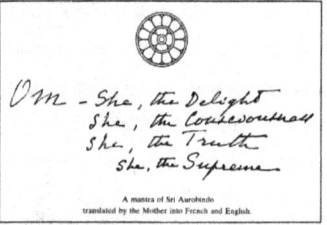 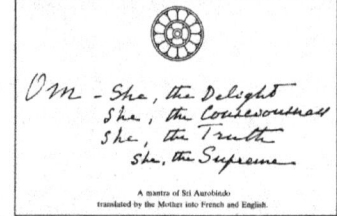

The first group of three gardens are meant to illustrate Brahman, the eternal Supreme Reality which is beyond time and space.

Second group of three gardens: Light, Life, Power
- *Light and Life* represent part of *the aspiring answer from matter* [to *Sat-Chit-Ananda*].
  - ➢ In her description of Sri Aurobindo's symbol, the Mother wrote that '*the ascending triangle represents the aspiring answer from matter* [to *Sat-Chit-Ananda*] *under the form of life, light and love*'.
  - ➢ In her comment for the flower she named '*Triple aspiration*', the Mother wrote: '*Love, Life and Light recognising their Master, respond to Sachchidananda.*'

- One may wonder why the Mother replaced here *Love* by *Power*, and what this particular *Power* is – considering that all gardens are *Powers*. What is actually this *Love* which is part of *matter's aspiring answer* [to *Sat-Chit-Ananda*]?

  On 21st January 1962, the Mother explained it while commenting on one of her visions:

  'It was like a memory, an eternally present memory of that consciousness of supreme Love emanated by the Lord onto earth – INTO earth – to draw it back again to Him. And truly it was the descent of the very essence of the divine nature into the most total divine negation, and thus the abandonment of the divine condition to take on terrestrial darkness, so as to bring Earth back to the divine state. And unless That, that supreme Love, becomes all-powerfully conscious here on Earth, the return can never be definitive.'

  Hence, *Love* is the *Power emanated by the Lord* into matter *to draw it back again to Him.*

- On 28th July 1861, the Mother described Max Théon's view of the first two manifestations:

  'The way Théon told it, there was first the universal Mother (he didn't call her the universal Mother, but Sri Aurobindo used that name), the universal Mother in charge of creation. For creating she made four emanations: Consciousness or Light; Life; Love or Beatitude and (Mother tries in vain to remember the fourth) ... I must have cerebral anaemia today! In India they speak only of three: Sat-Chit-Ananda (Sat is Existence, expressed by Life; Chit is Consciousness, expressed by Power; Ananda is Bliss, synonymous with Love). But according to Théon, there were four (I knew them by heart). Well, these emanations (Théon narrated it in such a way that someone not a philosopher, someone with a

childlike mind, could understand), these emanations, conscious of their own power, separated themselves from their Origin; that is, instead of being entirely surrendered to the supreme Will and expressing only.... Ah, the fourth emanation is Truth! Instead of carrying out only the supreme Will, they seem to have acquired a sense of personal power. (They were personalities of sorts, universal personalities, each representing a mode of being.) Instead of remaining connected, they cut the link – each acted on his own, to put it simply. Then, naturally, Light became darkness, Life became death, Bliss became suffering and Truth became falsehood. And these are the four great Asuras: the Asura of Inconscience, the Asura of Falsehood, the Asura of Suffering and the Asura of Death.

Once this had occurred, the divine Consciousness turned towards the Supreme and said (Mother laughs): 'Well, here's what has happened. What's to be done?' Then from the Divine came an emanation of Love (in the first emanation it wasn't Love, it was Ananda, Bliss, the Delight of being which became Suffering), and from the Supreme came Love; and Love descended into this domain of Inconscience, the result of the creation of the first emanation, Consciousness – Consciousness and Light had become Inconscience and Darkness. Love descended straight from the Supreme into this Inconscience; the Supreme, that is, created a new emanation, which didn't pass through the intermediate worlds (because, according to the story, the universal Mother first created all the gods who, when they descended, remained in contact with the Supreme and created all the intermediate worlds to counterbalance this fall – it's the old story of the 'Fall,' this fall into the Inconscient. But that wasn't enough). Simultaneously with the creation of the gods, then, came this direct Descent of Love into Matter, without passing through all the intermediate worlds. That's the story of the first Descent.'

- In the evolution first came Light, then came Life and with it the possibility for this Power to express itself and bring us back to our divine origin.

The second group of three gardens seem to represent the three Powers which the Universal Mother put into matter when she exteriorised her consciousness to create the universe. This in accord with Kireet Joshi for whom these three gardens are intimately linked to Chit (consciousness).

Third group of three gardens: Wealth, Utility and Progress

According to Kireet Joshi, these three are connected to Sat (Existence).

These three appear to be the Powers which are necessary for the divine fulfilment of life – which is the aim of Sri Aurobindo's Yoga (and not the release from life which is the aim of most other yogas). We have to learn how to produce more and different kinds of <u>wealth</u> and find ways to <u>utilise</u> these for a substantial <u>progress</u>. This requires a deep understanding and mastery of these three Powers.

Screening compost for a special soil mix

Fourth group of three gardens: Youth, Harmony and Perfection.
According to Kireet Joshi, these three illustrate Ananda (Bliss).

These three are both a means and an end. We all aspire to remain young and live in harmony and be surrounded by perfection; this would be Ananda. But for it to be possible, we have to manifest these Powers within ourselves.

On the names of the 1ˢᵗ group of 3 gardens: *Existence, Consciousness, Bliss*

About Existence, Consciousness and Bliss – the 1ˢᵗ group of 3 gardens:

Together the first 3 gardens represent Sachchidananda – the Supreme Being in eternity.

The names of the first 3 gardens are: *Existence* (Sat), *Consciousness* (Chit) and *Bliss* (Ananda); that is, Sat-Chit-Ananda (or *Sachchidananda*), which is the essence of the Divine.

A flower represents this triple power:
Sachchidananda (ref. No 3). Comment: *Strong and pure, it stands erect in its creative power.*

In a way, Matrimandir too represents Sachchidananda:
Before naming the *soul of Auroville 'Matrimandir'*, the Mother spoke of it as the *Pavilion of* Truth, the *Pavilion of* the Mother and the *Pavilion of [Divine]* Love. But, as we have seen[7] that:

Truth is also Existence.

The Mother is the Consciousness and Force of the Divine.

Love is a form of Bliss.

Hence Matrimandir itself represents Sachchidananda.

---

7. See the Annexure by the same author on *'Correlations between the names of the twelve gardens and other texts'*.

Relevant quotes:

God is Sachchidananda. He manifests Himself as infinite existence of which the essentiality is consciousness, of which again the essentiality is bliss, is self-delight. (Sri Aurobindo[8])

The Supreme is Pure being, Absolute Existence, sat...
The Supreme is also Pure Awareness, Absolute consciousness, cit...
The Supreme is, finally, Pure Ecstasy, Absolute Bliss, Ananda... (Sri Aurobindo[9])

That which has thrown itself out into forms is a triune Existence-Consciousness-Bliss, Sachchidananda, whose consciousness is in its nature a creative or rather a self-expressive Force capable of infinite variation in phenomenon and form of its self-conscious being and endlessly enjoying the delight of that variation. It follows that all things that exist are what they are as terms of that existence, terms of that conscious force, terms of that delight of being.
(Sri Aurobindo[10])

He is the one Existence: he is the original and universal Delight that constitutes all things and exceeds them: he is the one infinite Consciousness that composes all consciousnesses and informs all their movements; he is the one illimitable Being who sustains all action and experience; his will guides the evolution of things towards their yet unrealised but inevitable aim and plenitude. To him the heart can consecrate itself, approach him as the supreme

---

8 *The Upanishads,* SABCL 12:96
9 *The Upanishads,* SABCL 12: 16,17,19
10. *The Life Divine,* SABCL 18:92

Beloved, beat and move in him as in a universal sweetness of Love and a living sea of Delight. For his is the secret Joy that supports the soul in all its experiences and maintains even the errant ego in its ordeals and struggles till all sorrow and suffering shall cease. His is the Love and Bliss of the infinite divine Lover who is drawing all things by their own path towards his happy oneness.

(Sri Aurobindo[11])

The Eternal is the one infinite conscious Existence... It is an active force of Conscious Being which realises itself in its powers of Self-experience, its powers of knowledge, will, self-delight and self-formulation with all their marvellous variations.

(Sri Aurobindo[12])

About Existence – the 1st garden:

Central flower selected by the Mother:

<u>Psychic Power in Existence</u> (Ref. No 600)

Comment: *Manifold, imperious, irresistible in its understanding sweetness.*

(The Mother picked up this hibiscus from a tray full of flowers. Richard reminded Her that She had already named it *Psychic Power* and She added the word *Existence*.)

Kireet Joshi's recommends reading:

Sri Aurobindo's *The Life Divine*, Chapter IX, *The Pure Existent*.

When we withdraw our gaze from its egoistic preoccupation with limited and fleeting interests and look upon the world with

---

11. *The Synthesis of Yoga*, SABCL 20:76-77.
12. Quoted by Richard.

dispassionate and curious eyes that search only for the Truth, our first result is the perception of a boundless energy of infinite existence, infinite movement, infinite activity pouring itself out in limitless Space, in eternal Time, an existence that surpasses infinitely our ego or any ego or any collectivity of egos, in whose balance the grandiose products of aeons are but the dust of a moment and in whose incalculable sum numberless myriads count only as a petty swarm. We instinctively act and feel and weave our life thoughts as if this stupendous world movement were at work around us as centre and for our benefit, for our help or harm, or as if the justification of our egoistic cravings, emotions, ideas, standards were its proper business even as they are our own chief concern. When we begin to see, we perceive that it exists for itself, not for us, has its own gigantic aims, its own complex and boundless idea, its own vast desire or delight that it seeks to fulfil, its own immense and formidable standards which look down as if with an indulgent and ironic smile at the pettiness of ours. And yet let us not swing over to the other extreme and form too positive an idea of our own insignificance. That too would be an act of ignorance and the shutting of our eyes to the great facts of the universe...

Sri Aurobindo's *The Synthesis of Yoga*, Part II, Chapter I, *The Object of Knowledge*.

About Consciousness – the 2nd garden:

Central flower selected by the Mother:

Supramental Consciousness (Ref. No 569).

Comment: *Gloriously awake and powerful. Luminous, sure of itself, infallible in its movements.*

(The Mother picked up this hibiscus from a tray full of flowers and said: *This flower is very luminous* and asked how She had named it. She was satisfied with the flower and its name.)

Relevant quotes:

Consciousness is a fundamental thing, the fundamental thing in existence – it is the energy, the motion, the movement of consciousness that creates the universe and all that is in it – not only the macrocosm but the microcosm is nothing but consciousness arranging itself.

(Sri Aurobindo[13])

Consciousness is made up of two elements, awareness of self and things and forces and conscious-power. Awareness is the first thing necessary, you have to be aware of things in the right consciousness, in the right way, seeing them in their truth; but awareness by itself is not enough. There must be a Will, and a Force that make the consciousness effective.

(Sri Aurobindo[14])

About Ananda – the 3rd garden:

Central flower selected by the Mother:

Ananda (Ref. No 565)

Comment: *Calm, tranquil, equal, smiling and very sweet*[15] *in its truly simple austerity.*

(Richard reminded the Mother that She had already named a hibiscus *Ananda*. She said: *It will do to represent the garden of Bliss.*)

---

13. *Letters on Yoga*, SABCL 22:236

14. *Letters on Yoga*, SABCL 22:238

15. The Mother probably said 'douce' which may be translated as 'gentle' or 'sweet'. Hence the difference in the two books on the significance of flowers.

Relevant quotes:

Ananda is Beatitude, the bliss of pure conscious existence and energy... (Sri Aurobindo[16])

According to our own philosophy the whole world came out of ananda *and returns into* ananda, *and the triple term in which* ananda *may be stated is Joy, Love, Beauty. To see divine beauty in the whole world, man, life, nature, to love that which we have seen and to have pure unalloyed bliss in that love and that beauty is the appointed road by which mankind as a race must climb to God.*

(Sri Aurobindo[17])

Beauty is Ananda taking form – but the form need not be a physical shape. One speaks of a beautiful thought, a beautiful act, a beautiful soul. What we speak of as beauty is Ananda in manifestation.

(Sri Aurobindo[18])

Ananda is the secret delight from which all things are born, by which all is sustained in existence and to which all can rise in the spiritual culmination

(Sri Aurobindo)

Ananda is the very essence of the Brahman, it is the supreme nature of the present reality.

(Sri Aurobindo)

* * *

---

16 *The Upanishads,* SABCL 12:85
17 *The Hour of God and Other Writings,* SABCL 17:238
18 *The Future Poetry,* SABCL 9:491

On the names of the 2nd group of 3 gardens: *Light, Life, Power*

About Light – the 4th garden:

Central flower selected by the Mother:
Light of the Purified Power (Ref. No 606)
Comment: *Irresistibly simple in its power solely consecrated to the Divine.*

(The Mother pointed to a hibiscus which She had named *Purified Power*. She added the word *Light* to its name.)

Relevant quotes:

Light is primarily a spiritual manifestation of the Divine Reality illuminative and creative; material light is a subsequent representation or conversion of it into Matter for the purposes of the material Energy.

(Sri Aurobindo[19])

Light is not knowledge but the illumination that comes from above and liberates the being from obscurity and darkness.

(Sri Aurobindo[20])

Our sense by its incapacity has invented darkness. In truth there is nothing but Light, only it is a power of light either above or below our poor human vision's limited range.

For do not imagine that light is created by the Suns. The Suns are only physical concentrations of light, but the splendour they concentrate for us is self-born and everywhere.

---

19. *The Mother*, SABCL 25:83
20. *The Life Divine*, SABCL 19:944

God is everywhere and wherever God is, there is Light.

(Sri Aurobindo[21])

Even if there is much darkness – and this world is full of it and the physical nature of man also – yet a ray of the true Light can prevail eventually against a tenfold darkness. Believe and cleave to it always.

(Sri Aurobindo[22])

About Life – the 5th garden:

Central flower selected by the Mother:
Power of Consciousness (Ref. No 592)
Comment: *All the powers of controlling and dominating the lower movements of inconscient nature.*
(This hibiscus drew the Mother's attention.)

Other flowers whose name and comment may enlighten us on the meaning of *Life:*
Life energy (ref. No 389). Comment: *Powerful and manifold, meets all ends.*

Relevant quotes:
[Life energy], *life-force is not physical in itself; it is not material energy, but rather a different principle supporting Matter and involved in it. It supports and occupies all forms and without it no physical form could have come into being or could remain in being. It acts in all material forces such as electricity and is nearest to self-manifestation in those that are nearest to pure force; no material*

---

21 *The Hour of God and Other Writings*, SABCL 17:48
22 *Letters on Yoga*: SABCL 23:585

force could exist or act without it, for from it they derive their energy and movement and they are its vehicles.

(Sri Aurobindo[23])

About Power – the 6th garden:

Central flower selected by the Mother:
Aesthetic Power (Ref. No 609)
Comment: *Beauty is a great power.*

(Richard was wondering which of the many hibiscus with *Power* in their name the Mother would select and he was thinking of *Dynamic Power*, but significantly She chose this one.)

Relevant quotes:

Power means strength and force, Shakti, which enables one to face all that can happen and to stand and overcome, also to carry out what the Divine Will proposes. It can include many things, power over men, events, circumstances, means, etc. But all this not of the mental or vital kind, but by an action through unity of consciousness with the Divine and with all things and all beings. It is not an individual strength depending on certain personal capacities, but the Divine Power using the individual as an instrument.

(Sri Aurobindo[24])

Force is the essential Shakti; Energy is the working drive of the Force, its active dynamism; Power is the capacity born of the Force; Strength is energy consolidated and stored in the Adhar.

(Sri Aurobindo[25])

---

23 *The Upanishads*, SABCL 12:200
24 *Letters on Yoga*, SABCL 24:1203
25 *Letters on Yoga*, SABCL 24:1204

About Light, Life and Power – the 2nd group of 3 gardens:

In our 'Correlations between the names of the twelve gardens and other texts', we have seen that:

In Sri Aurobindo's symbol, *the ascending triangle represents the aspiring answer from matter* [to *Sat-Chit-Ananda*] *under the form of* life, light *and love*.

In the parable told by the Mother, God's first four emanations were: 1) Light *or Consciousness*, 2) *Ananda or Love*, 3) Life and 4) *Truth*.

In Théon's 'Cosmic square', Love was at the centre and was surrounded by might, light, life and utility. Mother replaced might (puissance) by Power (Pouvoir).

Flower representing at least part of this triple power:

Triple aspiration (ref No 124).

Comment: *Love, Life and Light recognising their Master, respond to Sachchidananda.*

According to Kireet Joshi, the names of these 3 gardens are intimately linked with Consciousness (Chit) and indeed, according to the above-mentioned correlations, it is God's consciousness (Chit), which emanated the first four emanations: Light *or Consciousness*, *Ananda or Love*, Life and *Truth*. *Love* is also one of the three forms under which matter answered to *Sat-Chit-Ananda*.

This is consonant with the 'Genesis' according to which God would have said: 'Let there be Light!' and chronologically Life indeed came after Light. The logic here seems to be clear.

But what about Power? What is this Power of Power?

Why did Mother replace *Love* with *Power* in this particular context? What does She mean by *matter's aspiring answer in the form of Love*? The idea of matter expressing love is not common.

As seen above, 'Puissance' (Might) constituted one of the four sides of Théon's 'cosmic square' but, for Matrimandir Gardens, the Mother replaced *Might* (Puissance) by *Power* (Pouvoir).

Note 1: The difference that exists between 'puissance' and 'pouvoir' is not exactly the same as that between 'might' and 'power'. For example in relation to an engine, 'puissance' is translated by 'power' and not by 'might'.

Note 2: The Mother gave to 45 flowers names with the word 'power' in it, and not a single one of these is about force; moreover She did not give to any flower a name with 'might' in it.

Note 3: One can speak of *'aesthetic power'* but not of 'aesthetic might'.

Note 4: Théon was an asura and for these beings and their puppets (such as Hitler and Stalin) 'might is right'. Sri Aurobindo and the Mother have fought against the rule of this barbaric principle whose time is now hopefully over and they brought down the power of the new consciousness which appears to be essentially an inner power to convince, convert and disarm – and not a power to impose by force. True power does not need force/might to impose itself.

The Mother did not want any imposition by force in Auroville, which is why She wrote: *No army, no police, no prison.*

The Mother explained that the 'new consciousness' does not want bloody wars and revolutions and indeed communist regimes all over Europe fell without the expected blood bath – and so did apartheid in South Africa.

Hence, in my view, what needs to be expressed in the Garden of Power is the Power of the Shakti, or *'matter's aspiring answer to Sachchidananda in the form of Love'* expressing itself by the power to convince, convert, disarm… that is to say in changing the consciousness of things and beings – which by the way is the purpose of evolution. *Aesthetic power*, the central flower selected by the Mother for this garden expresses very well this power. In my view again, nature's sometime brutal and irresistible force is not what should be evoked in the *Garden of Power*.

* * *

On the names of the 3rd group of 3 gardens: *Wealth, Utility, Progress*

About Wealth – the 7th garden:

Central flower selected by the Mother:

(The Mother asked Richard what was the flower for *Wealth*. He told Her that we have *Wealth* for water lilies and *Riches* for the cacti; but in French there is only one word 'Richesse' for both wealth and riches. She said that these flowers will do.)

Wealth (ref. No 548). Comment: *True wealth is that which one offers to the Divine.*

Supramental wealth (Ref. No 549). Comment: *Wealth placed at the service of the Divine.*

Wealth in the Mind of Light (ref. No 550). Comment: *Open to all higher ideas.*

Wealth under the psychic influence (ref. No 551). Comment: *Wealth ready to return to its true possessor, the Divine.*

Emotional wealth (ref. No 552). Comment: *The only true emotional wealth is love for the Divine.*

Wealth in the vital (ref. No 553). Comment: *Comes willingly to generous natures.*

Wealth in the most material vital (ref. No 554). Comment: *Can be stable only after conversion.*

Generous wealth (ref. No 555). Comment: *Likes to be given and spread far and wide.*

Integral Wealth of Mahalaksmi (Ref. No 556). Comment: *Wealth in all domains and all activities, intellectual, psychological, material, in feeling and action.*

Riches (ref. No 561). Comment: *It is the Divine to whom all riches belong. It is the Divine who lends them to living beings. It is He to whom they must naturally return.*

Supramental riches (ref. No 563). Comment: *Riches that are at the disposal of the supramental being and still unknown to man.*

Relevant quotes:

All wealth belongs to the Divine and those who hold it are trustees, not possessors. It is with them today, tomorrow it may be elsewhere. All depends on the way they discharge their trust while it is with them, in what spirit, with what consciousness in their use of it, to what purpose.

(Sri Aurobindo[26])

---

26 *The Mother with letters on the Mother,* SABCL 25:12

About Utility – the 8th garden:

Central flower selected by the Mother:
Usefulness of Auroville[27] (ref. No 590)
Comment: *A creation that aims at teaching men to surpass themselves.*
(The Mother chose this hibiscus.)

Relevant quotes:
Utility is about the proper use of things and what the Mother says below about the proper use of money can surely be said about the proper use of any form of wealth. (Underlines are the compiler's.)

Money is not meant to generate money; money should generate an increase in production, an improvement in the conditions of life and a progress *in human consciousness. This is its true use. What I call an improvement in consciousness, a* progress *in consciousness, is everything that education in all its forms can provide – not as it's generally understood, but as we understand it here: education in art, education in ... from the education of the body, from the most material progress, to the spiritual education and progress through yoga; the whole spectrum, everything that leads humanity towards its future realisation. Money should serve to augment that and to augment the material base for the earth's* progress, *the best use of what the earth can give – its* intelligent utilisation, *not the utilisation that wastes and loses energies. The use that allows energies to be replenished.*

In the universe there is an inexhaustible source of energy that

---

27. Also named: *"Usefulness of the New Creation".*

asks only to be replenished; if you know how to go about it, it is replenished. Instead of draining life and the energies of our earth and making of it something parched and inert, we must know the practical exercise for replenishing the energy constantly. And these are not just words; I know how it's to be done, and science is in the process of thoroughly finding out – it has found out most admirably. But instead of using it to satisfy human passions, instead of using what science has found so that men may destroy each other more effectively than they are presently doing, it must be used to enrich the earth: to enrich the earth, to make the earth richer and richer, more active, generous, productive and to make all life grow towards its maximum efficiency. This is the true use of money. And if it's not used like that, it's a vice – a 'short circuit' and a vice.

But how many people know how to use it in this way? Very few, which is why they have to be taught. What I call 'teach' is to show, to give the example. We want to be the example of true living in the world. It's a challenge I am placing before the whole financial world: I am telling them that they are in the process of withering and ruining the earth with their idiotic system; and with even less than they are now spending for useless things – merely for inflating something that has no inherent life, that should be only an instrument at the service of life, that has no reality in itself, that is only a means and not an end (they make an end of something that is only a means) – well then, instead of making of it an end, they should make it the means. With what they have at their disposal they could ... oh, transform the earth so quickly! Transform it, put it into contact, truly into contact, with the supramental forces that would make life bountiful and, indeed, constantly renewed – instead of becoming withered, stagnant, shrivelled up: a future moon. A dead moon.

We are told that in a few millions or billions of years, the earth will become some kind of moon. The movement should be the opposite: the earth should become more and more a resplendent sun, but a sun of life. Not a sun that burns, but a sun that illumines – a radiant glory.

(The Mother[28])

About Progress – the 9th garden:

Central flower selected by the Mother:

Power to Progress (ref. No 616)

Comment: *Precious because of its rarity, it must be cultivated with care.*

(Though there was already *Progress of Auroville* and *Power of Progress* the Mother chose this hibiscus. In answer to a question of Richard, the Mother said that *power to progress* and *power of progress* were not the same thing.)

Other flowers whose name and comment may enlighten us on the meaning of *Progress:*
- Progress (ref. No 283). Comment: *This is why we are on earth.*
- Power of progress (ref. No 615). Comment: *Progress is the sign of the divine influence in creation.*
- Progress of Auroville[29] (ref. No 587). Comment: *Each one must find the activity favourable to one's own progress.*
- Simple sincerity (ref. No 290). Comment: *The beginning of all progress.*
- Silence (ref. No 321). Comment: *The ideal condition for progress.*

---

28 *Mother's Agenda*, 04.10.58.
29 Also named: *"Progress of the New Creation"*.

- Vigilance (ref. No 416). Comment: *Indispensable for all true progress.*
- Dynamic Power (ref. No 610). Comment: *Indispensable for progress.*
- Vital patience (ref. No 740). Comment: *Indispensable for all progress.*
- Perfect quietness of the mind (ref. No 728). Comment: *Essential condition for true progress.*
- Purity in the emotional centre (ref. No 770). Comment: *Indispensable for progress.*
- Combined offering of two parts of the being (ref. No 154). Comment: *This heralds the progress and effectiveness of the being.*
- Integral renunciation of vital desires (ref. No 200). Comment: *An indispensable condition for true progress.*
- Work (ref. No 247). Comment: *Let us offer our work to the Divine – this is the sure way to progress.*
- Disinterested work done for the Divine (ref. No 250). Comment: *The surest way to progress.*
- Thirst to learn (ref. No 282). Comment: *One of the qualities that facilitate integral progress.*
- Plasticity (ref. No 397). Comment: *Always ready for the necessary progress.*

Relevant quotes:

The thirst for progress, the thirst to know, the thirst to transform yourself, and above all the thirst for Love and Truth – if you keep that, you go faster. Truly a thirst, a need, you know, a need. All the rest has no importance, what you need is THAT.

No more bonds – free, free, free, free! Always ready to change everything, except ONE thing: to aspire. That thirst.

The "Something" we need, the Perfection we need, the Light we need, the Love we need, the Truth we need, the supreme Perfection we need – and that's all. The formulas – the fewer the formulas, the better. A need, a need, a need... which only THE Thing can satisfy, nothing else, no half measure. Only That. And then, move on, move on! Your path will be your path, it doesn't matter; any path, any path whatever.

(The Mother[30])

Progress: the reason why we are on earth. (The Mother[31])

About Wealth, Utility and Progress – the 3rd group of 3 gardens:

Let us note that '*Utility*' was one of the four sides of Théon's 'cosmic square'.

According to Kireet Joshi, the names of these 3 gardens are intimately linked with *Existence* (*Sat*) and indeed *Wealth*, *Utility* and *Progress* are clearly connected. All wealth belongs to the Divine and have to be re-conquered for Him/Her. Utility is about finding the proper use of things – that is to stimulate progress at all levels.

As the Mother pointed out in the text on Utility and Progress reproduced on the previous page, the earth is presently being turned into a dead moon while if it could be *put into contact, truly into contact, with the supramental forces, that would make life bountiful and, indeed, constantly renewed – instead of becoming withered, stagnant, shrivelled up: a future*

---

30 *Mother's Agenda*, 07.10.64.
31 *Words of the Mother*, CWM 15:82

moon. A dead moon. Instead of that, *the earth should become more and more a resplendent sun, but a sun of life. Not a sun that burns, but a sun that illumines – a radiant glory.* These three gardens together illustrate the most pressing challenge of our time – the challenge which threatens our very existence.

* * *

On the names of the fourth group of three gardens: *Youth, Harmony, Perfection*

About Youth – the 10th garden:

Central flower selected by the Mother:

Beauty of Supramental Youth (ref. No 573)

Comment: *Exquisitely fresh and powerful with uncontested beauty.*

(The Mother liked the hibiscus *Supramental Beauty* but changed its name to *Beauty of Supramental Youth*.)

Other flowers whose name and comment may enlighten us on the meaning of *Youth:*

Spring purity (ref. No 312). Comment: *The charm and freshness of youth.*

Eternal youth (ref. No 580). Comment: *It is a gift the Divine gives to us when we unite with Him.*

Relevant quotes:

Youth does not depend on the small number of years one has lived, but on the capacity to grow and progress. To grow is to increase one's potentialities, one's capacities; to progress is to make constantly more perfect the capacities that one already possesses.

(The Mother[32])

---

32 *On Education*, CWM 12:259

To be young is to live in the future.

To be young is to be always ready to give up what you are in order to become what you should be.

To be young is never to accept the irreparable. (The Mother[33])

To know how to be reborn into a new life at every moment is the secret of eternal youth.

(The Mother[34])

About Harmony – the 11th garden:

Central flower selected by the Mother:

Power of Harmony (ref. No 608)

Comment: *Simple, noble, dignified, powerful and charming.*

(The Mother saw this hibiscus and named it *Power of Harmony*.)

Other flowers whose name and comment may enlighten us on the meaning of *Harmony*:

Harmony (ref. No 350).

Comment: *Let us work for the day when this will become both the means and the end.*

Integral harmony (ref. No 353).

Comment: *Harmony between things, harmony between persons, harmony of circumstances and, above all, harmony of aspirations – all leading towards the Supreme Truth.*

Relevant quotes:

For all problems of existence are essentially problems of harmony. They arise from the perception of an unsolved discord and the

---

33 *On Education*, CWM 12:122

34 *On Education*, CWM 12:124

instinct of an undiscovered agreement of unity. To rest content with an unsolved discord is possible for the practical and more animal part of man, but impossible for his fully awakened mind, and usually even his practical parts only escape from the general necessity either by shutting out the problem or by accepting a rough, utilitarian and unillumined compromise. For essentially, all Nature seeks a harmony, life and matter in their own sphere as much as mind in the arrangement of its perceptions.

(Sri Aurobindo[35])

It is only in union with the Divine and in the Divine that harmony and peace can be established. (The Mother[36])

About Perfection – the 12th garden:

Central flower selected by the Mother:

(The Mother herself suggested the flower *Psychological Perfection*, and added: *'all kinds'*.)

Psychological perfection (ref. No 664)

Comment: *There is not one psychological perfection but five, like the five petals of the flower: sincerity, faith, devotion, aspiration and surrender.*

Psychological perfection on the way to fulfilment (ref. No 665)

Comment: *The state of those who take up the Yoga seriously.*

Psychological perfection in matter (ref. No 666)

Comment: *The first step towards transformation.*

Integral psychological perfection (ref. No 667)

---

35 *The Life Divine*, SABCL 18:2
36 *Words of the Mother*, CWM 14:198

Comment: *One of the conditions indispensable for transformation.*

Perfect Psychological Perfection (ref. No 668)
Comment: *Psychological perfection in all parts of the being.*
Supramentalised psychological perfection (ref. No 670)
Comment: *A psychological perfection aspiring to be divinised.*

Other flowers whose name and comment may enlighten us on the meaning of *Perfection*:
Thirst for perfection (ref. No 662)
Comment: *Constant and manifold aspiration.*

Relevant quotes:
Perfection is not a maximum or an extreme. It is an equilibrium and a harmonisation.

(The Mother[37])

It may be said that perfection is attained, though it remains progressive, when the receptivity from below is equal to the force from above which wants to manifest.

(The Mother [38])

Such qualities as faith, sincerity, aspiration, devotion, etc, make up the perfection indicated in our language of the flowers. In ordinary language it would mean something else such as purity, love, benevolence, fidelity and a host of other virtues.
(Sri Aurobindo[39])

---

37 *Words of the Mother,* CWM 15:85
38 *Words of the Mother,* CWM 15:85
39 *Letters on Yoga,* SABCL 23:554.

We thirst for perfection. Not this human perfection which is a perfection of the ego and bars the way to the divine perfection. But that one perfection which has the power to manifest upon earth the Eternal Truth.

(The Mother[40])

The maximum a human being can attain just now is an equilibrium which is not progressive. He may attain perhaps a static equilibrium but all that is static can be broken for lack of progress.

Perfection will be attained in the individual, the collectivity, on the earth and in the universe, when, at EVERY MOMENT, the receptivity will be equal in quality and quantity to the Force which wants to manifest.

This is the supreme equilibrium.

(The Mother[41])

About Youth, Harmony and Perfection – the 4th group of 3 gardens:

According to Kireet Joshi, the names of these 3 gardens are intimately linked with *Bliss* (*Ananda*) and indeed, *Youth, Harmony* and *Perfection* surely are an excellent recipe for *Bliss* or its outcome.

One is also reminded of the Charter which speaks of *"a youth that never ages"*.

* * *

---

40 *Words of the Mother,* CWM, 15:186
41 *Questions and Answers 1950-51,* CWM, 4:16

Annexure: Correlations between the names of 12 Gardens and other texts

There are some interesting correlations between the names of the twelve gardens and some other texts written by Sri Aurobindo or the Mother. These correlations may help us better understand why the Mother listed these particular *Powers*. There are surely some other interesting texts.

Correlations between Sri Aurobindo's symbol and Matrimandir Gardens

The descending triangle represents Sat-Chit-Ananda.

The ascending triangle represents the aspiring answer from matter under the form of life, light and love.

The junction of both – the central square – is the perfect manifestation having at its centre the Avatar of the Supreme – the lotus.

The water – inside the square – represents the multiplicity, the creation.[42]

Correlations:

Sat-Chit-Ananda (*Existence, Consciousness, Bliss*), is the essence of the Divine and it is also the names given by the Mother to Gardens 1, 2 and 3 respectively.

Life and *Light* are the names of Gardens 5 and 4 respectively.

Love is represented by Matrimandir itself[43].

---

42 The Mother. (CWM)

43 The Mother had spoken at first of *Matrimandir* as the *Pavilion of Truth*, or *Pavilion of the Mother*, or *Pavilion of [Divine] Love*.

Matrimandir itself represents a lotus in full bloom and the *Mahashakti* or *Divine Consciousness*.

The Mother wanted water to surround Matrimandir and She also insisted on having running water.

* * *

Correlations between Max Théon's 'cosmic square' and Matrimandir Gardens

In January 1972, while trying to remember the names of Her 12 *Virtues*, the Mother told Satprem:

Did you read in the Cosmic Review about the 'cosmic square'?

1, 2, 3, 4, and one in the centre? The cosmic square was conceived by Théon[44], and I know he put Love in the centre. But the four sides ... what are the four sides? I don't remember anymore. I used to know all that so well; it's all gone. I know there was Light, Life, and Utility – the fourth was Utility, but the first? Utility was the last. What was the first? It's all gone. That would have given me a clue.

Correlations:

The name the Mother could not remember on that day is 'Puissance'[45] which should probably be translated in this particular context as 'Might'.[46]

Light, Life and *Utility* are respectively Gardens 4, 5 and 7 and *Love* (Matrimandir) stands at the centre of all twelve gardens.

---

44 Max Théon had been the Mother's instructor in occultism.
45 Théon's 'Revue Cosmique' was published in French.
46 For example, 'Dieu tout-puissant' is 'God almighty'.

The Mother did not name Garden 6 'Puissance' (Might) but *'Pouvoir'* (*Power*). We will come back on this subtle difference in our paper "On the significance of the twelve gardens".

* * *

Correlations between the parable of God's first four emanations and Matrimandir Gardens

One day "God" [whose essence is *Sat, Chit, Ananda*] *decided to exteriorise himself, objectivise himself, in order to have the joy of knowing himself in detail. So, first of all, he emanated his consciousness (that is to say, he manifested his consciousness) by ordering this consciousness to realise a universe. This consciousness began by emanating four beings, four individualities which were indeed altogether very high beings, of the highest Reality. They were the being of* consciousness, the being of love (of Ananda rather), the being of life and the being of light and knowledge – but consciousness and light are the same thing. *There we are then:* consciousness, love and Ananda, life and truth – *truth, that's the exact word. And naturally, they were supremely powerful beings, you understand. They were what are called in that tradition the first emanations, that is, the first formations. And each one became very conscious of its qualities, its power, its capacities, its possibilities, and, suddenly forgot each in its own way that it was only an emanation and an incarnation of the Supreme. And so this is what happened: when light or Consciousness separated from the divine Consciousness, that is, when it began to think it was the divine Consciousness and that there was nothing other than itself, it suddenly became obscurity and inconscience. And when Life thought that all life was in itself and that there was nothing else but its life and that it did not depend at all upon the Supreme, then its life became death. And when Truth thought that it contained all truth, and that there was no other truth than itself, this Truth became falsehood. And when love or Ananda was convinced that it was the supreme Ananda and that there was no other than itself and its felicity, it became suffering. And that is how the world, which was to have been so beautiful, became so ugly. Now, that consciousness (if you like to call it the Divine Mother, the Supreme Consciousness), when she saw this she was very disturbed, you may be sure, she said to herself: "This has really not succeeded." So she turned back to the Divine, to God, the Supreme, and she asked him to come to her aid. She said to him: "This is what has happened. Now what is to be done?" He said: "Begin again, but try to manage in such a way that the beings do not become so independent!... They must remain in contact with you, and through you with me." And it was thus that she created the gods, who were quite docile and not so proud, and who began the creation of the world. But as the others had come before them, at every step the gods met the others. And it was in this way that the world changed into a battlefield, a place of war, strife, suffering, darkness and all the rest, and for each new creation the gods had to fight with the others who had gone ahead: they had preceded them, they had plunged headlong into matter; and they had created all this disorder and the gods had to put straight all this confusion. That is where the gods came from. They are the second emanations...*

The story may be understood in a much more occult and spiritual sense...[47]

Light or Consciousness, Ananda or Love, Life and Truth. Then Light or Consciousness became Darkness and Inconscience. Love and

---

[47] The Mother, CWM Volume: 5 (Questions and Answers 1953), Page: 372-73.

Ananda became Hatred and Suffering, and Truth became Falsehood, and Life became Death.[48]

Hence, to recapitulate:
Truth (or *Knowledge*) *became Falsehood.* But *Truth* is also *Existence.*
Consciousness (or *Light*) *became Darkness and Inconscience.*
Love (*or rather Ananda*) *became Hatred and Suffering.*
Life became Death.

Correlations:
We find again *Light, Life and Love*, as was already the case with the ascending triangle in Sri Aurobindo's symbol and in Théon's *Cosmic Square*. It is now clear that these are the powers the Divine Mother (*the Consciousness and Force of the Divine*) manifested or exteriorised into matter.

---

48 The Mother, CWM, Volume 6 (Questions and Answers 1954), Page: 173.

4 November 2007

Narad issues an explanatory note on the MM Gardens:
On the significance of the order of the Matrimandir Gardens

I have occasionally been asked about the significance of the arrangement of the twelve Gardens of the Matrimandir. How do the Gardens relate to each other in the order that has been given by Mother?

The first Garden is the ***Garden of Existence***. All begins with existence, Sat, and I see this Garden as representative of the initial manifestation with its stone, pools, primordial plants such as bamboo, ferns, etc.

Planting Psychic Power in Existence in the Garden of Existence

Sri Aurobindo: "Existence is an infinite and therefore indefinable and illimitable Reality which figures itself out in multiple values of life." *Social and Political Thought*

"All existence, – as the mind and sense know existence – is manifestation of an Eternal and Infinite which is to the mind and sense unknowable but not unknowable to its own self-awareness." *The Hour of God*

"All existence is a manifestation of God because He is the only existence . . . ." *Essays on the Gita*

The second Garden is the **Garden of Consciousness**, the natural and divine progression after Existence. Chit.

Sri Aurobindo: "Consciousness is a fundamental thing, the fundamental thing in existence - it is the energy, the motion, the movement of consciousness that creates the universe and all that is in it - not only the macrocosm but the microcosm is nothing but consciousness arranging itself." *Letters on Yoga*

"To me, for instance, consciousness is the very stuff of existence and I can feel it everywhere enveloping and penetrating the stone as much as man or the animal. A movement, a flow of consciousness is not to me an image but a fact." *Letters on Savitri*

The third Garden is the **Garden of Bliss** with its representative flower a hibiscus, as are the flowers of the first two Gardens. In fact, the hibiscus carries such importance that it represents ten of the twelve Gardens of the Matrimandir.

Sri Aurobindo: "For from the divine Bliss, the original Delight of existence, the Lord of Immortality comes pouring the wine of that Bliss, the mystic Soma, into these jars of mentalised living matter; eternal and beautiful, he enters into these sheaths of substance for the integral transformation of the being and nature." *The Life Divine*

"And this bliss is not a supreme pleasure of the heart and sensations with the experience of pain and sorrow as its background, but a delight also self-existent and independent of objects and particular experiences, a self-delight which is the very nature, the very stuff, as it were, of a transcendent and infinite existence." *The Synthesis of Yoga*

So, the first three Gardens represent Satchitananda which leads us to the fourth Garden. As Sri Aurobindo has given us a luminous understanding of Satchitananda, more need not be said.

Of course, it will not be required that one go through all the Gardens in a consecutive manner, beginning with the ***Garden of Existence***. For, as Mother told me, in whatever Garden one enters one will feel, "physically and concretely the significance of each Garden. In the ***Garden of Youth***, they will know (Mother emphasized this word) youth, in the ***Garden of Bliss*** they will know bliss," etc.

The fourth Garden is the ***Garden of Light***, manifesting from Satchitananda. It too has as its representative flower, the hibiscus.

Sri Aurobindo: "... light is primarily a spiritual manifestation of the Divine Reality illuminative and creative; material light is a subsequent representation or conversion of it into Matter for the purposes of the material Energy." *The Life Divine*

"Our sense by its incapacity has invented darkness. In truth there is nothing but Light, only it is a power of light either above or below our poor human vision's limited range.

For do not imagine that light is created by the Suns. The Suns are only physical concentrations of Light, but the splendour they concentrate for us is self-born and everywhere.

God is everywhere and wherever God is, there is Light." *The Hour of God*

"Light is a general term. Light is not knowledge but the illumination that comes from above and liberates the being from obscurity and darkness." *The Mother*

"The light is everywhere, the force is everywhere. And the world is so small." *Words of the Mother,* MCW Vol. 15.

With the advent of *Light* there is *Life,* the fifth Garden of the Matrimandir Gardens. It is interesting to note that the *Garden of Life* is the closest Garden to the Banyan tree, the geographical centre of Auroville, and for me the symbol of Unity. On the western side of the Banyan are the twelve *Unity* Gardens. In fact, Mother said to me, "I would like you to begin with the *Garden of Unity.*" (Emphasis, mine.)

Sri Aurobindo: "Life itself here [on earth] is Being at labour in Matter to express itself in terms of conscious force; human life is the human being at labour to impress himself on the material world with the greatest possible force and intensity and extension." *Social and Political Thought*

"Life is the dynamic expression of Consciousness-Force when thrown outward to realise itself in concrete harmonies of formation." *Letters on Yoga*

"Life [is] not only a play of forces or a mental experience, but a field for the evolution of the concealed spirit." *Letters on Yoga*

"All life is only a lavish and manifold opportunity given us to discover, realise, express the Divine." *Social and Political Thought*

The *Garden of Power,* the sixth of the twelve *Gardens of the Matrimandir,* of which Mother has said, "The Gardens are as important as the Matrimandir." I see *Power* as the strongest force emanating from *Life,* and this Garden too is represented by a hibiscus.

Sri Aurobindo: "Power means strength and force, Shakti, which enables one to face all that can happen and to stand and overcome, also to carry out what the Divine Will proposes. It can include many things, power over men, events, circumstances, means, etc. But all this not of the mental or vital kind, but by an action through unity of consciousness with the Divine and with all things and beings. It is not an individual strength depending on certain personal capacities, but the Divine Power using the individual as an instrument."
Letters on Yoga

Planting an area of the Matrimandir Gardens

The seventh of the **Matrimandir Gardens**, the **Garden of Wealth**, is the inevitable result of *Power*. **Wealth** is one of the two Gardens represented by flowers other than the hibiscus. Its most significant flower is the water lily which, in the spiritual significances of the flowers given to us by The Mother, represents **Wealth**. The many colours of water lilies respond to the messages of the flowers in the hierarchy as given by Mother and Sri Aurobindo. Hence we have the following: **Supramentalised Wealth**, pink with a large golden centre, **Wealth in the Mind of Light**, blue with a large golden centre, **Wealth under the Psychic Influence**, white flowers shaded pink, **Emotional Wealth**, lavender flowers, **Wealth in the Vital**, vivid magenta pink flowers, **Wealth in the most material vital**, deep rose red flowers, **Generous Wealth**, yellow flowers, and **Integral Wealth of Mahalakshmi**, white flowers. These water lilies will be complemented by various cacti which represent *Riches*.

Sri Aurobindo: "All wealth belongs to the Divine and those who hold it are trustees, not possessors. It is with them today, tomorrow it may be elsewhere. All depends on the way they discharge their trust while it is with them, with what consciousness in their use of it, to what purpose." *The Mother*

"Wealth is a force — I have already told you this once — a force of Nature; and it should be a means of circulation, a power in movement, as flowing water is a power in movement. It is something which can serve to produce, to organise. It is a convenient means, because in fact it is only a means of making things circulate fully and freely. This force should be in the hands of those who know how to make the best possible use of it, that is, as I said at the beginning, people who have abolished in themselves or in some way or other got rid of every personal desire and every attachment. To this should be added a vision vast enough to understand the needs of the earth, a knowledge complete enough to know how to organise all these needs and use this force by these means. If, besides this, these beings have a higher spiritual knowledge, then they can utilise this force to construct gradually upon the earth what will be capable of manifesting the divine Power, Force and Grace. And then this power of money, wealth, this financial force, of which I just said that it was like a curse, would become a supreme blessing for the good of all.'" *Collected Works of the Mother* – Vol. 7.

"True wealth is that which one offers to the Divine." *Collected Works of the Mother* – Vol. 15.

The correct use of wealth leads to the next Garden which Mother named *Utilité*, which was originally translated as Utility and is now Usefulness. *Usefulness* is the eighth Garden of the Matrimandir and is again represented by a hibiscus.

The outcome of usefulness is naturally progress, which is the ninth Garden of the **Matrimandir Gardens**. The **Garden of Progress** is represented by a hibiscus and, as many of the Gardens, may also contain many of the 'companion' plants that bear similar significances such as Catharanthus (common name Vinca) which Mother named *Progress.*

Sri Aurobindo: "A spiritual atmosphere is more important than outer conditions; if one can get that and also create one's own spiritual air to breathe in and live in it, that is the true condition of progress." *Letters on Yoga*

"The first condition of inner progress is to recognise whatever is or has been a wrong movement in any part of the nature, - wrong idea, wrong feeling, wrong speech, wrong action, - and by wrong is meant what departs from the truth, from the higher consciousness and higher self, from the way of the Divine. Once recognised it is admitted, not glossed over or defended, - and it is offered to the Divine for the Light and Grace to descend and substitute for it the right movement of the true Consciousness." *Letters on Yoga*

Youth is the tenth Garden of the Matrimandir and surely, after passing through the previous nine Gardens and experiencing the states of consciousness they represent, we will see that *Progress* will bring us to an eternal *Youth*, in which there will be a continuing progress and unfolding of the wonders still unknown in which the rarest gems of the spirit will be revealed with the opening of the vaults of the soul.

The Mother: "Youth does not depend on the small number of years one has lived, but on the capacity to grow and progress. To grow is to increase one's potentialities, one's capabilities, one's capacities; to progress is to make constantly more perfect the capacities that one already possesses. Old age does not come from a great number of years but from the incapacity or the refusal to continue to grow and progress. I have known old people of twenty and young people at seventy." *On Education*, MCW Vol. 12.

The eleventh Garden of the Matrimandir is *Harmony*, that most elusive and important aspect of man's evolutionary journey to the Supreme. *Harmony*, too, has been chosen by Mother to be represented by a hibiscus along with other flower significances that vibrate with the Divine Harmony.

Sri Aurobindo: "When all is in agreement with the one Truth or an expression of it, that is harmony." *Letters on Yoga*

Lastly, we come to the twelfth Garden, the **Garden of Perfection**, represented by the Plumeria (common name Frangipani or Hawaiian Lei flower) with a few forms. There is *Psychological Perfection* bearing white flowers with a large yellow centre, *Psychological Perfection on the way to Fulfilment* with predominantly deep rose to purplish red flowers often shaded with deep yellow to orange, *Psychological Perfection* *in Matter*, with predominantly white flowers edged with rose pink, with a rose pink band on the back of each petal and a tiny yellow centre, *Integral Psychological Perfection* with large white flowers whose petals are widely separated, and finally *Perfect Psychological Perfection* with large white flowers with overlapping petals. One of the most beautiful companion plants will be ***Supramentalised Psychological Perfection***, the beloved and intensely fragrant *Michelia champaka*, commonly known as Champak.

Sri Aurobindo: "Perfection in the sense in which we use it in Yoga, means a growth out of a lower undivine into a higher divine nature. In terms of knowledge it is a putting on the being of the higher self and a casting away of the darker broken lower self or a transforming of our imperfect state into the rounded luminous fullness of our real and spiritual personality. In terms of devotion and adoration it is a growing into a likeness of the nature or the law of the being of the Divine, to be united with whom we aspire . . ." *The Synthesis of Yoga*

"Out of imperfection we have to construct perfection, out of limitation to discover infinity, out of death to find immortality, out of grief to recover divine bliss, out of ignorance to rescue divine self-knowledge, out of matter to reveal Spirit. To work out this end for ourselves and for humanity is the object of our Yogic practice." *Essays Divine and Human*

The Mother: "Perfection is not a maximum or an extreme. It is an equilibrium and a harmonisation." *Words of the Mother*, MCW Vol. 15.

"Perfection is eternal; it is only the resistance of the world that makes it progressive." *Words of the Mother*, MCW Vol. 15.

"It may be said that perfection is attained, though it

remains progressive, when the receptivity from below is equal to the force from above which wants to manifest." *Words of the Mother*, MCW Vol. 15.

And, as T.S Eliot writes in the last of his Four Quartets, **'Little Gidding'**...

"We shall not cease from exploration and the end of all our exploring will be to arrive where we started and know the place for the first time."

And so we arrive once again at *Existence*, the first principle of Satchitananda, and feel it concretely, know its significance in our very being as when we first entered, but now even more so having passed through all the states of consciousness that the other eleven Gardens have revealed to us.

Narad

February 2008

Alain Grandcolas writes to Narad setting out his personal responsibilities in the Matrimandir Gardens:

Dear Narad,

I understood from you that you are preparing a list of the work to be executed during your absence, and I approve of it. In this context, I like to define the responsibilities which I have assumed and like to continue to keep:
 1. Prototype of the various pathways of the gardens,
 2. Marking of the crests,
 3. Marking of all the levelings,

4. Development of designs for prototypes,
5. Development of prototypes.

I hope this definition of function will meet your approval,

Alain

undated

Note from Narad to Amrita

Dear Amrita,

I take it that you would not like to read their emails, so I won't send them. I really don't know how they found my address but I guess it is not too difficult these days. Shraddhalu told me he had a vision that if these people should prevail the Matrimandir would be taken down to the four pillars.

That's all for now, it is nearing midnight.

Narad

Response from Amrita to Narad:

Dear Narad,

What email treatises? And what is the "Matrimandir Action Committee"? As far as Kireet Joshi is concerned, whatever he may say, he has himself created many of the problems at Matrimandir. I don`t wish to elaborate on this, but this has been my observation. In fact, it has been my general observation that, aside from the stupidity, naivete, and inveterate obstinacy of the lower nature of those who call themselves Aurovilians, most of the political problems in Auroville have been directly created by those closest to the Mother, and the factions in Auroville have split exactly down the lines represented by these individuals. It`s not necessary to name them because I think you know all of them. I don`t wish to put the entire blame on them, but the fact is, that these individuals do shoulder a major part of the blame, because they did have a major part of the responsibility, power, authority and position bestowed upon them by the Mother. As such, they should have been examples to the rest of us of harmony, collaboration and goodwill expected of people who had done at least some sadhana. But the opposite happened. And frankly Kireet is no exception.

Otherwise, I`m quite happy and sometimes even blissful in my ignorance. And generally I don`t much want to know what is going on. Maybe "Ignorance is bliss" should be amended to "Detachment is bliss". I don`t know. The sweetness and happiness in one`s heart must be guarded like a precious jewel. It`s so easy for anything beautiful in this world to be destroyed. I suppose this is why roses have thorns.

Take care, I hope you feel better.

Love,

Amrit

Narad writes to Amrita:

For the moment I've misplaced August's address in Bangkok, but he will send it to you.

Amrit, you are always close to me no matter how far apart physically and are an integral part of Her work.

With my love and a warm embrace.
At Their Feet,

Narad

Amrita reply to Narad:

Dear Narad,

I hope you had a nice trip back and have settled back into your life in the U.S. after your stay here in Pondy. The pink cassias are now in bloom, and they`re wonderful. The *Cassia javanica* is in full bloom, and the *lancasteri* just starting. Perhaps because of the lack of rains last year, I think the blooming is a little less. Same for the plumerias. Heinz came and has more or less finished his work with photographing the plumerias. He showed me a tentative example of how it would be. It`s really something wonderful what he has done. We`ve also started to pay more attention to the plumerias you planted many years back outside the Nursery. We`ve cleaned it up and put thorn around it to help protect it, as villagers were breaking the branches and using the area for their night-time excursions. I must say that some of the crossings you have planted there have turned out to be really superb and exquisitely beautiful. Even though Heinz is very talkative, and previously I found him very draining, I`ve come to appreciate him much more, because truly speaking, I have almost no one with whom I can discuss anything about plants or learn anything, especially ornamentals, except perhaps Kabul. Kabul has been enormously helpful in the orchid propagation. Without him, we would have been at a loss.

I was happy also that you came, because it renewed an old contact and inspiration. I`ve felt for so many years that as far as the Nursery was concerned, it was nothing but dragging and trying to keep one`s head above water - so much opposition, inertia, and plain bad will. Somehow I feel much better now about the Nursery, with the renewed contact with you, with Heinz, the trip to Nong Nooch. I think slowly things will pick up. In fact, within a few months, probably Heinz and I will take a trip to Sri Lanka and Thailand for some plants. And of course, an added factor in the improved mood has been the distancing of myself from my former responsibilities and Matrimandir politics.

At present what I`m doing is going through all the plants in the Nursery, correcting whatever mistakes there were in the lists, identifying what had not been identified, and making a list of all the unidentified plants. With this, Zulfi is compiling a list of all the flowers and plants that might be put in each Garden, with all the relevant data pertaining to each plant (situation, type of plant, blooming period, suitability for beds or pots, etc). I`m happy with him, because up to now I could not find anyone to help with this type of work. We`re still going on the assumption that there will be gardens, and that what The Mother wills, will be. In the meantime, I think it is very important to continue quietly one`s work.

To get to another point, if we go to Thailand, I would like to know the addresses of both Daniel and Hoos in Thailand, and their emails if possible. And maybe you could tell me a little of what they`re doing there, and would they at all mind if I tried to contact them?

Hope all is well with you,

Love,

Amrit

Undated

Note on the Banyan tree

Our Sacred Banyan by Narad

If you were to ask me, 'What are the two most sacred trees in the world today?' I would answer without hesitation, 'The Service Tree over the Samadhi of Sri Aurobindo and the Mother and the Banyan Tree at the centre of Auroville.' It was in 1968 (or at the latest 1969) that Mother gave me the work of caring for the Service Tree for the rest of my life. It is an inestimable blessing carrying with it a great responsibility, and it is in this light and with the same sense of devotion that I speak of the Banyan Tree.

My observations are not intended to criticize any person or group, so I shall not mention names, but will try and give an accurate assessment of the condition of the tree and the extensive work that needs to be done to keep it a strong and healthy symbol of Auroville's aspiration for unity. I am in India this year until March 2nd when I return to the U.S. However, most of the critical work on the Banyan can be accomplished in that time. I will be working with Juan, a professional tree pruner from Barcelona whom many of you already know. We met on January 16th and are in complete and harmonious agreement on every essential point of the work to be done.

Perhaps I can begin with the problem of the grass under the Banyan. It is certainly attractive but it has led to serious problems, one of the most serious is that frequent watering may have contributed to the fungal condition now in the central trunk. I first heard something about the fungus in the early 1990's and do not know when the grass was planted, but if it was not the initial cause it is most probably a contributing factor creating the ideal environment for the spread of the disease. I am not a tree surgeon familiar with the diseases of tropical trees, but I have spoken to the team at the Matrimandir and suggested that they begin to search for a qualified person in India or Sri Lanka, Singapore or Thailand to make a determination as to the possibility of a cure.

Juan made a cryptic comment that holds deep significance. He said, 'Grass is not the friend of trees.' I'll expand on his statement in a few areas. The first is the unchecked growth of the tree. I saw a photo of the Banyan taken in 1975. Its estimated diameter was twenty metres, a very good size for a tree that had been hacked for years by the village goatherds who fed their animals the leaves and aerial roots. We began protecting and caring for the Banyan in the early1970's when the first housing was built at the centre. Some of the older

Aurovilians may remember the village lady who slept under the tree to protect it and the experience Mother related of the tree coming to Her and telling her that a workman had put an axe or similar cutting instrument in its trunk. We measured the tree the other day and its diameter is now fifty metres, an increase of thirty metres in twenty-eight years! The eastern side of the tree is now at the edge of one of the western petals. It is not difficult to calculate what could happen if this rate of growth is allowed to continue. In the tropics where we have a twelve month growing season trees need their periods of dormancy, allowing the soil to dry out according to the climatic conditions prevalent in an area. Constant watering disrupts their natural cycle. One may cite seeming exceptions to this in England, Europe and the U.S. where there are beautiful rolling lawns and landscapes dotted with magnificent trees. However, these are areas where there is an enforced dormancy due to frost and freezing weather and a growing season of 4-6 months (frost-free) is often considered generous. Even in the warmer zones of the southern U.S. the same grass as under the Banyan, St. Augustine, grows under trees since it is possibly the most shade tolerant species. These areas experience ample rainfall almost monsoon-like at times, but St. Augustine is an aggressive species susceptible to fungal attacks and other diseases. Landscape companies fertilize heavily and frequently apply strong chemicals to control disease and insects.

The next problem is the root system. The first rule in tree culture is to water deeply but infrequently to encourage the roots to move down into the earth eventually finding their own sources of water. In Lewis Carroll's 'Through the Looking Glass', Alice asks the flowers if they can talk. They reply (and

I paraphrase) 'Of course we can talk, when there is anyone worth talking to'. Trees are very conscious even though they cannot express themselves in mental terms, and those of us who have lived close to them for a lifetime can tell you that they have taught us quietly about their work on earth and are shining examples of the aspiration for light. Trees are also not at all averse to keeping their roots at ground level or slightly below and taking advantage of free water at the surface. This is why they often go into shock when someone who has been watering the grass goes on vacation or forgets to water, or an irrigation system breaks down, and suddenly a tree which has not developed a deep root system becomes severely stressed, shedding leaves and weakening, a condition favourable for the onset of insects and disease. There is also the problem of tissue necrosis that occurs when people pile soil on top of the roots to create a shade garden with annual flowers. This is a rather fast way to kill a tree. There is a delicate ecosystem at work in the root system with millions of beneficial micro-organisms, macro-organisms, oxygen transporters, etc. If one disrupts this by mounding soil on the roots it can lead to early death.

The Banyan is a strong tree and survives great periods of drought and is able to grow under varied climatic conditions, but when it has been force-fed for years and its aerial roots indiscriminately encouraged to take root, things become a lot more precarious. For this reason I would not recommend removing the grass immediately, except perhaps for the inner area around the main trunk. I would suggest rather that a conscientious and carefully monitored spacing out of the watering period be initiated. For example (and I don't know the watering schedule at the present time) if watering is once a week, extend this to once every ten days for a period of weeks. Then over another period space out watering to every fourteen days, and so forth, so as not to put the Banyan under further stress. Keep extending the period between watering to determine the minimum amount of water needed by the grass. At this point a decision can be made as to whether to continue with minimal watering and keep the grass, or remove it. I would recommend removal. For centuries people have meditated on the soil of Mother India and mats can easily be supplied on special occasions.

The question we should take up next is that of the aerial roots which were put down without any serious study of the needs of the tree. It was reported to me that one of the persons in charge of the project said they put many roots down to see how they developed and then they would cut down those not needed. I'm afraid that I see this as a cruel and harsh approach and one that is without question horticulturally unsound. I never prune more than is necessary, and if there is extensive pruning to be required I undertake that in stages, again to stress the tree as little as possible. I would not recommend that anyone encourage further aerial roots to descend without serious study of the necessity of such roots for the support of essential branches. There are so many aerial roots to be removed now that I hope this will never happen again. One has only to look at those that have been put down next to the main trunk! Again, one has only to observe the size that some of these roots have attained and one can see that many of them if not removed now would grow into each other, creating an impenetrable wall in the future and one that would be totally lacking in beauty, to say the least. One of the aerial roots closest to the main trunk has become so large by taking up vast amounts of water that it is now threatening to dominate the main trunk. We do not feel that anything can be done about this, but perhaps an expert in Ficus could advise us.

Mary Helen and I travelled all throughout India and saw the great banyans in Calcutta, at the Theosophical Society in Chennai and in other tropical areas, and observed their beauty and their problems. Our Banyan has numerous limbs with extensive rot and decay that have never been attended to in the twenty-three years I have been away. These will have to be cleaned out and some of them removed. Many of these limbs are now eclipsed by dense growth above and have no place to develop. Yet they have had aerial roots artificially induced.

Lastly, some people have commented about the metal ring around the Banyan. Could there not be another place for the ring to be displayed, freeing the Banyan from the feeling of constriction and allowing it to express the flowing beauty of the mother trunk?

One must keep in mind the proportion of the Banyan to the Matrimandir and the perspective and balance of the entire area. We need to keep the Banyan in good health as a strong symbol of Auroville along with the Matrimandir and the Matrimandir Gardens, for our children and generations to come. The goodwill and prayers of all Aurovilians will be of much help to those who have to carry out the work.

Narad

February 2010

Correspondence with Sraddhalu Ranade of the Sri Aurobindo Ashram:

Dear Sraddhalu,

All can be undone, even the walkways. From a horticultural perspective alone, what has been done is violently against Nature. First, against my strong objection and that of others, including experts on Ficus benghalensis (the Banyan) contacted by Noel, they put one foot of soil over the whole area to achieve the level Roger wanted. When he spoke to me I told him not to do this. He then asked me if we could put just four inches of soil, and I said that could be done without changing the relationship of oxygen transport that the tree had developed over decades, but not to put soil up against the main trunk or other large trunks. I have seen so many beautiful trees killed in the West by people who recently moved into a home and thought, "Let's make a flower garden". They would get good soil and compost, manure, and other soil additives and put about one foot of soil all around the tree, right up to the trunk. In a few years they would see their beautiful tree dead from necrosis of the tissue caused by suffocation of the roots and the drastic change of the layers of microbial action, water percolation and oxygen transport. I am no expert in explaining these things but have witnessed too much devastation through unconscious treatment of Nature. Finally, Roger's team found someone (I believe it was Paul at the "Botanic Garden" whom I believe is an expert) who said there would be no harm done in filling the area with one foot of soil. What have they gained? Why would one take the chance? The water now stays near the trunks during the monsoon and who knows what kind of rot will occur as the years progress. At least they kept the soil away from the trunks. But the feeling of the beauty and the balance is gone and all this for wanting the rain to drain away properly, which it does not. Then, there is the damage that was done for the twenty years that I was away after Navajata's thugs nearly killed me. Mary Helen brought me directly from the hospital (with my head wrapped in bandages after my head was stitched) to Nolini's room, and after blessing me he said, "Take no part in all of this". I have held to this all these years.

Note the size of the Banyan in relation to the Matrimandir

When I left in 1981, Divakar, Arjun and Co. took over as the Matrimandir coordinating team. Against all common sense they planted a lawn under the Banyan, a tree that is completely adapted to its environment of long periods of drought followed by monsoon rains. I have seen the great banyan in Calcutta, another banyan covering about an acre in the Theosophical Society in Chennai, and there was just sandy soil beneath, no lawn. Now, all that watering allowed the tree to grow to three times its size in 1972. When I returned after Mary Helen's passing, I had to carefully and consciously see that the tree was pruned so that we would still have an area for the Garden of Life and a bit more room for the Garden of Power. Without pruning there would no longer be an area for the Garden of Life. Also, if the tree had continued to receive water, its roots would probably be breaking some of the Petals. To add to the disaster of those years, whenever there was no work, Arjun and Divakar would send the workers to the Banyan and tell them to put down more aerial roots.

When I returned I met a man from Spain, a professional tree pruner, Juan, who has helped me since then with pruning the serious break of the Service Tree limb over Mother's room, the Neem tree just opposite the Ashram gate in front of Kailashbhai's room, and a large pruning job at Arabinda Basu's house, and never has asked for any money.
I have also found work for him elsewhere as the Rs. 4,500 per month was not sufficient to support him and his child. After I interviewed Juan for fifteen minutes I found that there was such harmony in our understanding of Nature and in our own natures that I asked Gilles Guigan to give him maintenance immediately. He did so (I believe this was the first time it was ever done at Matrimandir) and Juan worked in complete harmony with me for three years and did excellent work on all the trees in the 'Park' surrounding the Matrimandir that I had planted more than thirty years ago. Now many of these trees will be destroyed when the 'Lake' is built. I asked if there could at least be islands to save some of them. Let us see. I am repeating constantly the names and asking, 'Thy Will Be Done'.

At this time the Banyan tree looked like a prison. The unnecessary and unconscious, almost hostile act, of putting down so many aerial roots totally destroyed the beauty of the Banyan. The first work Juan and I did was to remove as many as possible. On the day we planned to remove them Jittu, Amrit and a few others came and sat on benches. Jittu told Juan and me that if we did this we would suffer pain that we could not imagine, and those with him began to invoke forces to harm or destroy us. Juan's whole body was shaking. I told him that he need fear nothing as I was calling Mother and She would protect us. As we began the work big Vladimir from the Matrimandir came and stood between Jittu, Amrit, and the others. Then many Auroville women began coming each day and standing as a shield against this group's hostile invectives. Then Roger came the next day as well as the Secretary of Auroville and offered their full support and the work was completed. The Secretary at the time told us not to worry about anything as he would dispatch the police if needed. At the end we counted the aerial roots we removed. There were twenty-eight. We then counted the aerial roots remaining. There were twenty-eight. We had not counted before as our concentration was exclusively on determining what aerial roots had no function and those that were needed to support the large branches.

Now what is being done is, in my humble opinion, a serious desecration. The area where rain falls from the outer branches of a tree is called the 'Drip Line'. This is where the greatest concentration of 'feeder' roots, the roots that supply water and nutrients to the tree, are located. What they have done is to pour reinforced concrete over these roots, then add Agra stone, and then put heavy granite benches on top of that. In addition to all of this, the soil is already slightly alkaline and the cement adds lime to make it even more alkaline, again disturbing the natural environment of the tree. If these 'abominations' are not removed I am concerned that the tree will suffer. I know that banyans are very strong trees and that Mother will not allow it to die, but what is being done is without any concern for the health of the tree, only a blind and fanatical adherence to implementing Roger's last wishes. This will also not be the end for he told me of his vision of a 'Children's Wonderland' where there would be streams made of gold and fish hanging from the trees and the children would happily play. Where is the Peace that Mother wanted in this area? And where is the peace and silence where one could sit and meditate under the Banyan? And have I mentioned to you that at the end of one of my meetings with Mother She said to me, "I would like you to begin with the Garden of Unity"?

Mother also told me and Anie that She wanted us to have the first house at the centre called Peace, and that She would ask Navajata to build it. He, of course, had no intention of doing it.

Now the present plan for the Garden of Unity is to have metal structures like sails to shade people sitting in the twelve sections, with rods holding the sails. Though many of us asked that small trees be used, they have instead filled the centre areas of the six sections with concrete once again, and now are making a concrete ridge (that will never be seen) as a separation between the two sections of each of the Unity areas. When I told Jacqueline that we could do all this with plants adhering to Roger's plan, but instead of grass we would plant Sri Aurobindo's Compassion on one side and another beautiful but low plant on the other side, and that there was no need for a partition as the crest could be realised with flowering plants, She spoke in the next meeting about the painful nights she had spent thinking of what we planned to do.

There is so much concrete and stone in the Matrimandir area. Mother wrote to Mary Helen in reply to her experimenting with Japanese Gardening techniques in a tropical environment, "Naturally it will be in the Japanese way". Mary Helen had mistakenly written Auroville Gardens instead of Matrimandir Gardens (though there were no Auroville Gardens at the time) and this is used against the Gardens team. I could have had all the pathways planted in a low maintenance grass or a fine gravel on which one could easily walk such as at Versailles, or many other options, but now they are laying down concrete and Agra and very costly coloured stones, for which they asked earmarked donations and received the money, so it had to be spent on exactly what Roger wanted! Already the stones are coloured with red soil and the initial intent is lost.

Well, this has turned into quite a long letter, but I wanted to give you some clear background in writing for whatever may happen in the future. I know that you will use the information discreetly, or openly if warranted, and you have my complete trust to use it as you feel.

With my love,
At Their Feet,

Narad

11 February 2010

Sraddhalu wrote:

Dear Narad,
So I hear from many who live in Auroville also! My only solace is that most of these things can be undone later. But I am told the concrete walkways may not be undoable. I hope enough people in Auroville can wake up in time.

With love,

Sraddhalu

11 February 2010

Narad writes to Sraddhalu:

Subject: Confidential - Banyan

I feel that I should tell you in all frankness and humility that what is being done under and around the Banyan is a sacrilege and an abomination.

In Their Love,

Narad

14th March 2016

Can the teaching of the Cosmic Tradition help us understand better the meaning of the names of some of the 12 gardens of Matrimandir?

By Gilles Guigan

Names given by Mother to these twelve gardens:
On 23.6.65, when she described the plan of Her future town to Satprem, Mother spoke of it having at its centre a *Pavilion* which she later named *"Matrimandir"*:

So in that park [at the centre of the town] I had seen the "Pavilion of Love" (but I don't like to use that word because men have turned it into something ludicrous); I am referring to the principle of divine Love. But it has been changed: it will be the "Pavilion of the Mother"; but not this [Mother points to herself]: the Mother, the true Mother, the principle of the Mother. (I say "Mother" because Sri Aurobindo used the word, otherwise I would have put something else – I would have put "creative principle" or "realising principle" or ... something of that sort.)

On 28th February 1968, a poster mentioned the word *Love* with regard to *Matrimandir* and listed the names (original French) of the twelve gardens which are to surround the Matrimandir, starting from the East radial and rotating counter-clockwise:
Existence, Conscience, Bliss,
Light, Life, Power,

Wealth, Usefulness,[49] *Progress,*
Youth, Harmony, Perfection.

Note that Mother selected *"Aesthetic Power"* as the central flower of the garden of "Power" and that it doesn't express any brutal might but a subtle power.

* * *

In order to understand the true meaning of the names of the first 3 gardens: Existence, Conscience, Bliss, it is crucial to know their Sanskrit names: Sat, Chit, Ananda, and to know that together they are the essence of the Divine. Without this knowledge, the words: *Existence, Conscience, Bliss* simply cannot express the depth of the meaning of *Sat, Chit, Ananda.*

* * *

In this article, we wonder whether the teaching of the Cosmic Tradition and Hebrew can help us better understand the true meanings of the names of 4 gardens whose names we highlighted: Light, Life, Power, Utility – and of [Divine] Love which is represented by Matrimandir. Why:

In Her description of Sri Aurobindo's symbol (which was earlier used by the Cosmic Tradition, with very minor differences), Mother wrote:

"The descending triangle represents Sat-Chit-Ananda.

The ascending triangle represents the aspiring answer from matter under the form of life, light and love.

---

49 "Utilité" can be translated as "Utility" as well as by "Usefulness". Richard Pearson (Ashram) feels it should be translated by "Usefulness" because the name of the central flower selected by Mother for this garden is "Usefulness of Auroville". I fully agree with him.

The junction of both – the central square is the perfect manifestation having at its centre the Avatar of the Supreme – the lotus.

The water inside the square represents the Multiplicity, the Creation."

In January 1972, while trying to remember the names of Her 12 Virtues, which She needed for to name the rooms in Matrimandir's 12 "petals", Mother told Satprem:

Did you read in the Cosmic Review about the 'cosmic square'?

1, 2, 3, 4, and one in the centre? The cosmic square was conceived by Théon, and I know he put Love in the centre. But the four sides ... what are the four sides? I don't remember anymore. I used to know all that so well; it's all gone. I know there was Light, Life, and Utility – the fourth was Utility, but the first? Utility was the last. What was the first?... It's all gone. That would have given me a clue.

According to our research, *"Power"* was the word Mother couldn't remember at that moment:

In the herewith attached article "On Numbers" from the Revue Cosmique, Max Théon wrote that "One is the symbol of love", "Two is the number of life", "Three is the symbol of light", "Four is the symbol of power" and "Five is the symbol of utility".

In the February 1906 issue of the "Revue Cosmique", Max Théon wrote:

"Th (numériquement 400) indique le quaternaire: la vie (ou vitalité) la lumière ou intelligence, la puissance et l'utilité qui voilent et manifestent le Pathétisme dans les Matérialismes."

"Th (numerically 400) indicates the quaternary: life (or vitality), light or intelligence, might and utility which hide and manifest the Pathetism in the Materialisms."

In the booklet "Un séjour chez les grands initiés" ("A sojourn at the great initiates"), in which Claire Themanlys[50] recounts her stay at the Théons at Tlemcen, in Algeria, she wrote:

«Tlemcen, vers l'est, est nimbé de brume matinale ; le fin minaret rose de la mosquée élance vers le ciel sa petite tour carrée, couronnée d'un nid de cigognes. Ary songe à d'autres tours carrées, plus hautes encore... A celle du haut, de laquelle, dans le passé lointain, Ebonnoh, en contemplation, entrait en rapport avec les Intelligences Libres. Il entend, en sa mémoire, l'écho des récits sublimes donnés par ses initiateurs dans les Livres Cosmiques ; il médite cette page du CHALDÉEN : « J'ai gravi la tour carrée, la tour à quatre angles. C'est à l'est, au nord, au sud et à l'ouest que sont les quatre angles. Par le pouvoir des forces de l'Amour, et de la Vie, de la Lumière et de la Puissance, qui, par évolution, sont prêtes pour la manifestation utile, j'ai grandi un à un les degrés en approfondissant leur secret...»

The last three sentences translate: "I climbed the square tower, the tower with four angles. The angles are facing east, north, south and west. By the power of the forces of Love, Life, Light and Might, which by evolution, are ready for the utilitarian manifestation, I grew one by one up the steps, while deepening their secrets."

Is it "Power" or "Might"? Theon and his English wife, Mary Chrystine, spoke English and their words were

---

50 Louis and Claire Themanlys were the friends of Mother's brother, Mattéo, through whom Mother came into contact with the Mouvement Cosmique, its publications and Max Theon and his wife.

translated in French by their devoted Teresa whose French was poor, according to Mother. We believe that Theon said "Power" and that Teresa translated it wrongly as "Puissance" instead of "Pouvoir". Why? Because, in most cases, "Power" should be translated as "Pouvoir" but the "Power of a motor" is translated as the "Puissance d'un moteur".

Knowing what Théon wrote about the meaning of number 5, may help us better understand what has to be expressed in the garden of "*Utilité*", "*Utility*":

"The number FIVE is the fifth number in degree and order of perfection, being the number or symbol of utility.

For all, the animal kingdom must, for utility, possess brain, with its network of nerves; blood, the physical nourisher; muscles, instruments of movement; veins, conductors or channels of the blood; and flesh, the shield or covering.

All vegetables also, for utility, must possess root, stem (with its branches), leaves, blossom, and fruit (with its seed).

All minerals also for utility, must possess, or be capable of possessing, purity, ductility, malleability, tenacity and durability.

Therefore FIVE is the symbol of utility. And herein is the fifth mystery.

Now a mystery is that which is hidden, as it were, a secret. As things become clear to knowledge and understanding, they cease to be mysteries; all things are governed by fixed laws and all laws of nature are simple because the infinite, the Pure Spirit, is simple, as laws of man are complex because he is himself in a state of complexity."

Undated

The Matrimandir Gardens - an experience of initiation

Some fifteen days ago, the *News & Notes* published a letter from a participant of the recently held Matrimandir Gardens Seminar calling for "gardens to make you feel welcome, cozy, comfortable, relaxed" and stating that the present concept does not give enough space for shady areas for strolling, for resting, for gathering and for meetings like the seminar which was held under the Banyan tree.

The Auroville city has been designed with 55% of the area allocated for green spaces (in addition to the Green Belt). These green spaces include parks and gardens meant, amongst others, for a stroll, resting, or small gatherings. However, the Matrimandir Gardens have a completely different purpose.

The 12 Matrimandir Gardens are not meant for strolling or for leisure as in a traditional garden, not meant for contemplation as in a Japanese Zen garden, but for experiencing the twelve states of consciousness in an environment which maintains a visible connection with the Matrimandir as part of an initiation and preparation.

There will be trees and plenty of shade in the Inner Park area, which is as big as the 12 Gardens areas, and plenty of shade in the two plots in which children will meet with the wonder and the unexpected in a Dream Land. The 12 Matrimandir Gardens will indeed have limited places with shade (although there will be some shade in the outer areas near the lake where small trees may be provided).

No efforts were made and are planned to be made to design "sinuous alleys and paths" as suggested, since the Mother has seen and approved the model of the Matrimandir

Gardens with straight paths. Most modules and objects used in the gardens are flexible and mobile to allow the gardens to evolve.

The work of the Matrimandir Gardens Reflection Team is a work of discovery and experimentation while maintaining some basic guidelines and principles. All who would like to participate in this spirit are invited to contribute through their work.

Alain G.

24.3.19

Note on the Matrimandir Gardens

By Richard Eggenberger

Sri Aurobindo spoke of a perfect perfection and indeed the Matrimandir Gardens will exemplify this for it is the Divine who is building them and they will be built exactly according to the Divine Will. In fact, they are already built in the subtle world and only await manifestation on the physical plane.

18.2.22

Letter from Don Cox, who worked with Narad in the very early days

Hi Narad,

In the early 2000s you contacted me about the Service Tree at the Ashram and a branch decay issue. I never heard back, how did that turn out? I hope the tree is still alive and well. It was existing in some very compromised growing conditions.

I have been out of touch with Auroville and Ashram contacts for many years, but recently was contacted by Julian Lines from Matagiri in New York, with whom I had worked in the mid 70s with the US based Auroville International. He has forwarded my info to an arborist there named Island and we have just exchanged emails. I'm happy to see photos and videos of the reforestation in Auroville that has taken place since you initiated the bunding and tree planting and gardens. I ran the Allis Chalmers tractors and hauled water and compost for your initial tree planting projects. I've seen some photos and videos. It's come a long way in 50 years.

I'm semi-retired, living in Chiang Mai, Thailand, with my Thai wife. I do some local consulting, but mostly remote advisory for tree care associates in the San Francisco region; assistance with diagnosis of tree problems, soil fertility, plant nutrition and pest/disease management recommendations; and I author arborist reports along with my 'boots on the ground' associates there who send me photos and descriptions.

I'm always open to collaboration on tree health care, soil fertility and tree management issues.

I hope you are well. Best wishes, Don

(Don Cox aka The Tree Doctor)

International Publications

Auroville Architecture
by Franz Fassbender

Auroville Form Style and Design
by Franz Fassbender

Landscapes and Gardens of Auroville
by Franz Fassbender

Inauguration of Auroville
by Franz Fassbender

Auroville in a Nutshell
by Tim Wrey

Death doesn't exist
The Mother on Death, Sri Aurobindo on Rebirth
Compiled by Franz Fassbender

Divine Love
Compiled by Franz Fassbender

Five Dream
by Sri Aurobindo

A Vision
Compiled by Franz Fassbender

Passage to More than India
by Dick Batstone

The Mother on Japan
Compiled by Franz Fassbender

Children of Change: A Spiritual Pilgrimage
by Amrit (Howard Shoji Iriyama)

Memories of Auroville - told by early Aurovilians
by Janet Feran

The Journeying Years
by Dianna Bowler

Auroville Reflected
by Bindu Mohanty

Finding the Psychic Being
by Loretta Shartsis

The Teachings of Flowers
The Life and Work of the Mother of the Sri Aurobindo Ashram
by Loretta Shartsis

The Supramental Transformation
by Loretta Shartsis

**The Mother's Yoga - 1956-1973 (English & French)
Vol. 1, 1956-1967 & Vol. 2, 1968-1973**
by Loretta Shartsis

Antithesis of Yoga
by Jocelyn Janaka

Bougainvilleas PROTECTION
by Narad (Richard Eggenberger), Nilisha Mehta

Crossroad The New Humanity
by Paulette Hadnagy

Die Praxis Des Integralen Yoga
by M. P. Pandit

The Way of the Sunlit Path
by William Sullivan

Wildlife great and small of India's Coromandel
by Tim Wrey

A New Education With A Soul
by Marguerite Smithwhite

Featured Titles

Divine Love

The texts presented in this book are selected from the Mother and Sri Aurobindo.
"Awakened to the meaning of my heart. That to feel love and oneness is to live. And this the magic of our golden change, is all the truth I know or seek, O sage."

Sri Aurobindo, Savitri, Book XII, Epilog

A Vision by the Mother

On 28th May 1958, the Mother recounted a vision she once had of a wonderful Being of Love and Consciousness, emanated from the Supreme Origin and projected directly into the Inconscient so that the creation would gradually awaken to the Supramental Consciousness. The Mother's account of this vision was brought out a first time in November 1906, in the Revue Cosmique, a monthly review published in Paris.

A Dream – Aims and Ideals of Auroville
the Mother on Auroville

50 years of Auroville from 28.02.1968 - 28.02.2018
Today, information about Auroville is abundant. Many people try to make meaning out of Auroville – about its conception, to what direction should we grow towards, and, what are we doing here?

But what was Mother's original Dream and what was her Vision for Auroville back then?

Matrimandir Talks by the Mother

This book presents most of Mother's Matrimandir talks, including how she conceived the idea for this special concentration and meditation building in Auroville.

Memories of Auroville - Told by early Aurovilians

Memories of Auroville is a book about the very early days of Auroville based on interviews made in 1997 with Aurovilians who lived here between 1968 and 1973. The interviews presented in this book are part of a history program for newcomers that I had created with my friend, Philip Melville in 1997. The plan was to divide Auroville's history into different eras and then interview Aurovilians according to their area of knowledge.
Our first section would cover the years from 1968 till 1973 when the Mother was still in her physical body.

The Way of the Sunlit Path

May The Way of the Sunlit Path be a convenient guide for activating this ancient truth as a support for a Conscious Evolution.
May it illumine the transformation offered to us in the Integral Yoga.

A Dream Takes Shape (in English, French, Hindi)

A comprehensive brochure on the international township of Auroville in, ranging from its Charter and "Why Auroville?" to the plan of the township, the central Matrimandir, the national pavilions and residences, to working groups, the economy, making visits, how to join, its relationship to the Sri Aurobindo Ashram, and its key role in the future of the world. This brochure endeavours to highlight how The Mother envisioned Auroville from its inception, some of the major achievements realised over the years, and some of the difficulties currently faced in implementing the guidelines which she gave.

Mother on Japan

I had everything to learn in Japan. For four years, from an artistic point of view, I lived from wonder to wonder. And everything in this city, in this country, from beginning to end, gives you the impression of impermanence, of the unexpected, the exceptional... ...everything in this city, in this country, from beginning to end, gives you the impression of impermanence, of the unexpected, the exceptional. You always come to things you did not expect; you want to find them again and they are lost – they have made something else which is equally charming.

Auroville Reflected

On 28 February 1968, on an impoverished plateau on the Coromandel Coast of South India, about 4,000 people from around the world gathered for a most unusual inauguration. Handfuls of soil from the countries of the world were mixed together as a symbol of human unity. Why did Indira Gandhi, the erstwhile Prime Minister of India, support this development for "a city the earth needs?" Why did UNESCO endorse this project? Why does the Dalai Lama continue to be involved in the project? What led anthropologist Margaret Mead to insist that records must be kept of its progress? Why did both historian William Irwin Thompson and United Nations representative Robert Muller note that this social experiment may be a breakthrough for humanity even as critics commented, "it is an impossible dream"?

A House For the Third Millennium
Essays on Matrimandir

Nightwatch at the Matrimandir...
A cosmic spectacle; the black expanse above, the big black crater of Matrimandir's excavation carved deep into the soil. The four pillars - two of which are completed and the other two nearing completion - are four huge ships coming together from the four corners of the earth to meet at this pro propitious spot...

Passage to More than India

This book is a voyage of discovery. In 1959 the author, Dick Batstone, a classically educated bookseller in England, with a Christian background, comes across a life of the great Indian polymath Sri Aurobindo, though a series of apparently fortuitous circumstances. A meeting in Durham, England, leads him to a determination to get to the Sri Aurobindo Ashram in Pondicherry, a former French territory south of Madras.

www.ingramcontent.com/pod-product-compliance
Lightning Source LLC
LaVergne TN
LVHW010317070526
838199LV00065B/5591